PEGGY AND JOHN

A WONDERFUL LIFE

PEGGY AND JOHN
A WONDERFUL LIFE

John Skelton

Book Guild Publishing

Sussex, England

First published in Great Britain in 2015 by
The Book Guild Ltd
The Werks
45 Church Road
Hove, BN3 2BE

Typesetting in Garamond by
YHT Ltd, London

Printed and bound in Spain under the supervision of
MRM Graphics Ltd, Winslow, Bucks

A catalogue record for this book is available from
The British Library.

ISBN 978 1 909984 88 2

This book is dedicated to a very special person, my late wife Peggy. In all our sixty-six wonderful years together, she never thought about herself first; it was always the family, and then herself. All those who were privileged to meet her simply loved her. No one will ever take her place or will she ever be forgotten. I miss her every minute of every day.

John Skelton

Peggy aged 20 years

Nanny – you were kind, gentle and caring with a remarkable inner strength; you were the heart of the family. Love you always Nanny, forever in our thoughts.

A loving Granddaughter Gemma, Steven and HJ

Acknowledgements

I would like to say thank you to those people who have helped me in writing this book. I couldn't have done it on my own.

First of all to Melissa's friend Karen, because she was the one who actually sowed the seed. I was talking to her one day some time ago now and telling her the story of my life. She said to me, 'What you should do, without any doubt, is write a book because you obviously had a fascinating life.' A few days later she sent me an e-mail and in the e-mail she wrote this in capital letters: 'YOU MUST WRITE THAT BOOK, YOU HAVE A BIG STORY TO TELL.' So, thank you Karen.

Then I have to thank Jackie Driscoll, who replied to my advert many months ago for someone to help with typing and putting my story onto the computer. She was the first one to reply. She came to meet me and asked if she could bring her mum with her, and of course I said she could. I know that both Jackie and her mum have done a tremendous amount of work in putting right my mistakes. I get a little bit confused, as I'm not a young person, and they always hold my hand and guide me through the trials of working on such a lengthy book. All the words in the book are mine, but Jackie has been in the background and a huge help to me, and so what I'd like to do is to give her a big hug.

Last but not least I must thank my four wonderful children, because from time to time I have had to refer to them for dates and times and to check that I have got things in the right sort of sequence. Not that they know everything that is in the book itself, but they have been a great support to me. So, Martin, Roland, Lesley and Jackie, thank you.

It has been difficult to write this book, but it has been made so much easier by these lovely people who have helped me over these many months.

1

It is some time since I felt that I had a story to tell about my life. After listening to some of my stories a few people had suggested to me that I should put pen to paper. When I began I did not know if it would turn into a whole book or just be committed to paper for my family and friends to read. I know that I have had a wonderful life, particularly after I met and married a very special person named Peggy. Together we had a lovely family and then we had a dream retirement together. However, nothing lasts forever, and I lost this very special person on the 28th of September 2010, after sixty-six years of happy marriage.

Now, I have to go back to the beginning which is of course my birth date 22 April 1924. I want to say a little bit about my grandparents because they had a great deal to do with my upbringing. My grandfather Alfred Wood was born in the East End of London and fought in the Boer War in South Africa; he was also in the 1914/18 war. Between those two wars he met and married my grandmother Ellen Jane Alderton. Between them they had four children, four daughters in fact, one was Gladys, one was my mother Ellen, next was Florence and then Lilian who we all called Aunt Ciss. My grandfather worked as a plate layer on the railway and they moved him from Stratford to Felixstowe, to a tied house which belonged to the railway in the High Road on the outskirts of the town of Felixstowe.

I'll tell you a little bit more about Gladys later on, but here I will continue with the other three daughters, Ellen my mother, Florence and Lilian. They used to get their entertainment by going to the Saturday night dances in the RAF station in Felixstowe. It was a large station and I understand that my mother was a very good singer. She was also a very good dancer and certainly her Charleston was one to watch and admire. All three of the girls met and married airmen. My father's name was Christopher Skelton and he actually came from Edinburgh. He met and married my mother in 1921 when she was only 17, although she put 19 on the wedding certificate. I think he would have been about 23, because in the 1911 Census he was put down as a 13-year-old boy.

From this marriage there came three children: my sister Gladys was born in 1922, I came along in 1924 and my brother Alf in 1925. We lived in Felixstowe at number 11 Felix Road but I have no recollection at all of living there. I also have absolutely no recollection of ever seeing my father; I couldn't tell you what he looked like or how he spoke. I don't remember talking to my father or hearing any conversation between my mother and my father, although I must have known of course he was in the RAF at that particular time. When I was maybe three or four, I'm not sure of the exact age, I was suddenly back living with my grandfather and grandmother in their railway terrace. Apparently my father had walked out of the marriage, never to be seen or heard of again.

Actually it's not quite true to say he was never heard of again, because of what happened many years later. My son Martin did a lot of hard work tracing our Scottish ancestry and he found that my father died of leukaemia in 1940. Martin found where he was buried; unfortunately it turned out to be a pauper's grave. I will tell you a little bit more about my Scottish ancestry later, when I come to that time of my life when I was able to travel with Martin back to Scotland. We went to many parts of Scotland where the name of Skelton was apparently well known in those years.

And so the three children, Gladys, myself and Alf, came under the control of my grandfather and grandmother, because my mother had to work. She worked in a laundry, ironing all day long in a very steamy atmosphere, and so we saw very little of her really, until of course she came home from work. My grandfather was a wonderful man who, had he been educated, would have been some remarkable person indeed. He had the knack of being able to talk to you and to tell you about life, and explain simply exactly what the world was made of. He was in the control of my grandmother. She was the matriarch and she managed the finances, and she was one of those people who were always able to influence the whole atmosphere of the house. Of course in the 1930s times were extremely hard for those people without employment or who were in irregular employment. My grandfather was lucky in as much as he worked for the railway and so he had a consistent income. All that was necessary really was to manage the budget and live within the income, and my grandmother was very good at that. There was no television, there was no radio, no telephone, no instant communication between people, and so my grandfather spent his time gardening. He was a very good gardener. He had a large back garden and he also had two allotments. He was the sort of person who was always digging or hoeing or doing something or other in the garden, and so we were lucky in that we were never short of food. The question of what we were going to eat the next day was never an issue because there were always plenty of vegetables and all sorts of fruits that grew in the garden.

When I was eight, there came another baby into the family. This was a big surprise. I can honestly say that I had no idea that my mother was pregnant, in fact I didn't even know that she had a boyfriend or that she was in any way attached to anyone other than her children and of course her mother and father. It's not surprising, I suppose, that it came out of the blue. I said before that as children we had very little to do with my mother – it was our grandmother and grandfather who were in charge and they were actually mother and father to us. I can't honestly remember what my mother looked like or how she acted, or her being in any way responsible for our behaviour – it seems strange when I look back on such a period. It certainly was strange that a baby should appear. His name was Robert (Bobby) James Skelton but who his father was I did not know. Bobby maintained in later life that Christopher Skelton came back for a short time and there was an association. I don't know how he knows this but he seems to think that was the case, and from that association he was produced. I have to say that he has some grounds for thinking this, because when you look at the photographs of my brother Alf with my grandfather along Felixstowe promenade and at the photograph of Bobby and my grandfather along the same promenade you could hardly identify which one is Bob and which one is Alf. There is a definite similarity in the way both of them look, the colour of their hair, everything about them, so who knows. Life went on and my mother, my grandmother and grandfather never spoke about it for the rest of their lives. Bobby never found out anything. It was a strange thing to happen to anybody, but there it is. He was a baby and therefore didn't actually fit in to our gang of friends as Alf and I were somewhat older.

Now I want to talk a little bit about Gladys Wood. If you remember, my grandfather and grandmother had four daughters. My mother was the second daughter and Gladys was the eldest, although they were born in the same year, 1903, Gladys in January and my mother in December. Once again you have to remember that this part of my tale is something which I didn't know at the time, because I was not yet born, but as it was discussed very much later in my life I have remembered the facts. As I have said, the three girls found their entertainment in going to the dances at the RAF station, where it would appear that Gladys fell in love with a young man named Reg Collins. He lived in Walton on the Naze, his family were bakers and confectioners and they had a shop in the High Street. I know nothing about the family at all other than where they lived. In 1922 Reg Collins' mother and father, his brother and sister and Reg himself emigrated to New Zealand.

We have the passenger list of the ship they travelled on, which sailed from Southampton to Wellington, although Wellington was not where they ended up. They settled in a small town called Putaruru in the north island of New

Zealand. Apparently my grandfather was devastated that it was Gladys's intention to follow Reg and emigrate to New Zealand, which she did. Martin cannot find the ship that she sailed on, or the date of her emigration – we think it was in 1924, purely and simply because my sister once told me that my mother said to her that the shock of it all brought on my birth. From time to time Gladys wrote to her father and it wasn't very long, as far as I understand it, before she was desperately homesick. She married in 1925 and by 1933 she had had five children – apparently each time she was hoping she could return she fell pregnant again. Her first child was a Down's syndrome child and that must have played heavily on her mental state.

Then the bombshell came – the letter which told my grandmother and grandfather that Gladys had committed suicide. That was in 1933, she jumped off a bridge into a river and her body was found further downstream. We do have the newspaper reports of this particular event, a very sad story. Gladys was in a bad state, not physically but mentally, and she left behind five children the last two of whom were twins and only a year old. I can't say much more about that particular period with regard to Gladys Wood, but later on in the book I will be able to tell you a great deal of the consequences of her emigration, her life in New Zealand and exactly where she committed suicide. This is because in my eighty-eighth year I did in fact go to New Zealand, about which I will say more later.

2

My first recollection of anything at all really was my first day at school when my teacher told me to sit down and be quiet; even then I was obviously a lad who was a little bit boisterous! I always remember her, as she was a tall lady, very stern and her name was Mrs Jones. It is the first real recollection I have – everything else so far has been drawn from things I have heard from other people. I was very happy at school, I enjoyed school life and I was always up for any fun or games. My school reports start from the age of eight in 1932; they always appear to be in my favour and don't suggest somebody who didn't like school. I was always a good writer. I was also decent with my sums and so all my school reports, right up until I left school, were reports that you could show anybody with some sort of pride.

Two or three doors away from where Alf and I lived there was a boy named Bob Keeble, he was two or three years older than me and so we became a gang of three. Bob Keeble was in charge, with me second in command. Bob Keeble's word would count for everything. Many times I was in conflict with my grandmother when I would say, 'But Bob Keeble says ...' She would reply, 'Never mind Bob Keeble, just do what I say.'

We lived in one of a row of cottages. There was a back path running the whole length of the row, each house had a large garden and at the bottom of our garden was a stile, which led on to a long row of small trees and bushes, perfect for making camps and fires, etc. The other side of this was twenty-five to thirty yards of cut grass, then the railway line, followed by the train platform for Felixstowe town. We were well known to the railway staff, who often told my grandfather of our misdemeanours. Of course, Alf and I were never sitting indoors; we were always out somewhere, quite often getting into mischief although it was always of a mild nature. However Bob Keeble was another matter. His father had many ferrets, and a shotgun, because he used to catch rabbits and sell them around the houses. I remember quite clearly that they were a sixpence each and he used to skin them on the spot; my grandmother was a regular customer. One day Bob Keeble got a hold of this shotgun. We tied Alf up against a tree and shot him with the gun, why I have no idea. The facts came out at bath time when the marks could be seen on his chest. Another torture involved putting his toe through an old-fashioned mangle, and we also put a fork through his big toe. Under Bob Keeble's instructions of course, and we simply had to carry them out. My time came when we had a bonfire and Bob Keeble told me to run though the ashes, which I did. However I was wearing rubber plimsolls at the time, which caught fire. Unfortunately this meant I spent a few weeks sitting on a mattress outside the back door with very bad blisters on my feet.

In the 1930s Felixstowe was a very posh, upmarket, seaside resort. The beaches would be full of nannies looking after children, and plenty of upper class people visited the town. There was a regular tennis competition when the likes of Fred Perry and Bunny Austin would compete. It was also the place where Mrs Simpson and the then King Edward did their courting, and as we now know that caused the king to abdicate. Then during the summer periods, particularly on Saturdays, people would arrive at the train station with their luggage. We made a wheelbarrow, which we were able to use to ply our trade taking people's luggage to their hotels or boarding houses. Of course we were not very popular with the taxi drivers, but it was all good fun and from time to time quite lucrative. The school holidays were totally different – we would go out in the morning and come back at night time. My grandparents knew that we would come home when we were hungry. I can only say there was so much to do, the boating pond, crabbing, looking for lobsters and finding old balls misdirected on the golf course, and swimming. The most exciting of all activities was to go aboard the Cork lightship which was some two miles out to sea.

Along the promenade at Felixstowe there were several people who had motorboats and they would be plying their trade off the promenade for either a trip around the harbour or out to the Cork lightship. I was well known to one or two of the boat owners, particularly one for whom I used to pump out the water from his boat's bilge. He used to give me a free trip every now and again out to the lightship, I might stay out there with the crew maybe for half a day or so and they used to feed me. I would then come back on a later boat. It was always a very nice experience for me. I wasn't with my brother at these times – for some reason or another, I don't know, he didn't always come down to the beach with me. I was one of those who spent the whole of the summer doing something or other on the beach.

The other thing that we used to do, and we did this together, was to go to the church which was towards the promenade. Once a month the RAF band had a service. The band used to march the airmen up to the church and then, when the band came out, my brother and I used to follow behind and march with them all the way down to the RAF station, which I can tell you was a long, long way. In mileage I couldn't say, but we enjoyed it. Another Sunday pastime would be walking with my grandfather, and you'll see the photograph of him with my brother and me on Felixstowe promenade. We would always have to be well dressed, we had to pull our shoulders back, we had to have our ties on and our socks pulled up and walk straight, no slouching. He was a military man, a musketry instructor and a sergeant in the First World War, so of course he was able to drill men and he drilled us in the same manner. We always had to look as though we were marching as opposed to strolling along a promenade. Another thing he used to do with us from time to time was what was called 'walking the line'. Felixstowe had three stations – Felixstowe town, Felixstowe pier and Felixstowe beach – and on some Sundays he used to have to go along the line with a fairly large mallet. If any of the blocks on the line were coming a little loose, he used to have to tap them in to tighten them up. Both myself and Alf would go along with him when it was his turn to do that sort of duty.

John, Grandad and Alf. Very smart!

I can only say that my time in Felixstowe was always one of looking forward, and personally not looking back. I know that my mother and my grandparents were always worried about what we were eating, because we knew the shops we could go into and always get a stale sandwich or a stale bun, we were well known in that respect. I know that when I told my mother this story later on in life she certainly didn't believe me, but I can tell you that it's perfectly true, in as much as we were not afraid of picking something up, an apple which had only been half eaten for instance. We would take it out of the gutter, take it down to the sea, wash it up and eat it. It was of no great worry to us who had eaten it before and we certainly never had a stomach upset. My mother never believed the story but I can tell you that it is perfectly true.

On Saturdays, both Alf and I were regular supporters of Felixstowe Town Football Club. We were in fact quite well known at the club. Of course we never actually paid to get in, we always went to the end of the ground and jumped over the fence. We were quite happy to just mix with the crowd. We were not the only boys to jump over that way, and I'm sure that the officials knew, but they never took any notice of that misdemeanour. Felixstowe were quite a good semi-professional team and were well supported. The highlight of the season would be a local derby against Walton which was a village just outside Felixstowe – they played in a cup game once a year, some sort of hospital cup I think. I can tell you that the games were not really like football matches, they were more like wars. Felixstowe Town themselves were the superior team, but you know what happens when people are playing a cup title, it is a tremendous leveller. This was certainly the case when games took place at the Walton ground which was like playing on a mud heap, as opposed to the Felixstowe ground which was perfectly cut and roped off, etc. But there it is, it was a well-known fixture and well reported in the papers at the time.

In the early part of 1932 two Scotsmen knocked on my grandmother's door, asking if she took in lodgers. They had been referred to her from the police station which was opposite the house. They had travelled down from Glasgow with their toolboxes and had found employment building a new water tower in Walton. One was named Dan Murray, the other I simply cannot remember his name and neither can any of my family members. I do not know for one moment how we all had accommodation in my grand-mother's house, although through the whole of my childhood, right up until the time I joined the navy at seventeen, it was not unusual to have three people in the same bed, and sometimes two beds in the same room. Dan Murray and his friend had one room; one supported Rangers, the other

Celtic, and they put their respective flags up on the bedroom wall. I remember nothing else about them at all. I guess they went to work and came home, and what they did with their time I have no idea. However, there must have been an association with my mother and Dan – certainly not recognised by me – for on 4 March 1933 they got married. Dan Murray became my step-father, and he, my mother, Gladys and Bobby moved to Harwich. Alf and I stayed with my grandparents in Felixstowe. What I did not realise at the time was that my mother was pregnant, and Brian was born in June 1933.

I continued to enjoy my childhood at Felixstowe – it never seemed to rain, and we always seemed to have a blue sky as I remember it. I enjoyed school, and out of school both Alf and I went out and about and did not need any money as we always found plenty to keep us occupied. We were both very good footballers and sport of any kind came quite naturally to us. After I left Felixstowe to go to Dagenham, my brother Alf became the schoolboy champion of Suffolk at the hundred-yards hurdle.

One incident stands out in my mind. I was considered to be a good actor and singer, and at a particular concert I was chosen to sing an important solo part. After the concert a very irate mother wanted to know why her son, who had been training to be a singer, did not get the part. Well, what an almighty commotion! I cannot remember, throughout the whole of my school life, my parents or guardians coming to any concert or play, and also when I was captain of the school football team, not once did anyone come to see me play. At the time it did not seem to bother me, in fact I hardly thought of it at all – only in later years, when I was the father of four children, did I take any interest in education. Both Peggy and I attended all sorts of activities and certainly went to parents' evenings. I then realised just what I had missed as a child. When I left primary school in 1935 the final remarks made, and I still have a copy of the report, said, 'Conduct excellent, good in all subjects. John works splendidly and is a very helpful boy,' this being signed by the head teacher.

My mother moved from Harwich and went to live in Stratford, East London. From there she moved into a house in Dagenham, 310 Parsloes Avenue, a well-known address to our family. My grandmother and grand-father, along with Alf and me, went on holiday in 1935 and we stayed at Parsloes Avenue, I think fairly soon after my mother lived there. I don't remember quite what happened during that week or so, but I do know that I enjoyed the comradeship that I got from other boys in that street. I was always keen on playing football, and so was Alf, and we were always ready for the rough and tumble of living in Dagenham. And so how it came about

I am not sure, but at the end of this holiday I stayed with my mother in Dagenham and did not go back to Felixstowe. Bobby, who had been living with my mother in Dagenham, went back to Felixstowe. That meant that in Felixstowe would be my grandmother and grandfather, Alf and Bobby. Only Gladys, Brian and I were then left in Dagenham. I'm not really sure now of the date when Doreen actually came, but it was sometime in February 1935. Arrangements had to be made for me to go to school and so I went to Halbett Street Senior Boys' School, an elementary school which you left at the age of fourteen.

I enjoyed my school days there, but I can't say that I enjoyed the life that I was leading in Dagenham, because it was totally different from the life that I had experienced in Felixstowe. You have to remember that those were the days of the Depression, hunger marches and things like that, and Dagenham was very different from Felixstowe – they were at opposite ends of the spectrum. Dan, my stepfather, was a good man, and he tried his best to stay in employment – he was a skilled carpenter and joiner – but unfortunately with the Depression and with the type of work which he did, well if it was raining and he was working outside then he was put off, and from time to time a job would finish and he would then have to start looking for other employment. Money was very short and I can assure you that it was difficult to put food upon the table. Of course as far as clothing was concerned, then we continued pure and simply to wear what we'd got – there was very little money spent on new clothes.

I didn't feel deprived at the time, but looking back I realise that we were struggling. Not the only ones, as there were many families who were struggling, we were no different from anybody else. As I have said previously, those people who had regular employment were considered to be the lucky ones. For instance there was a man who lived on the opposite side of the road to us and he was just a bus conductor, but because he had this regular employment he was considered to be one of the well-off people. The main body of children were, in fact, those from backgrounds which were struggling to keep themselves alive.

One of my tasks, when I got to maybe twelve or thirteen, was to get up at about three o'clock in the morning and go out with another lad who lived opposite us. He went by the name of Lang – he picked up the name of 'chicky' Lang, how he got that I don't know. We used to catch the milk float and go up to the shopping centre on Green Lane, which was a fair way away, where it was our job to call into the bakeries there and buy two or three pennies' worth of stale bread and any cakes that were available. Sometimes we were lucky at the first shop, sometimes we had to walk on and go into two or three until we made a purchase and brought the products home. I also had a paper round in the morning and another paper round at night, which used to bring in some money, but of course getting up at three o'clock for the bread, then doing the paper round, then going to school and then coming home and doing the evening paper round, it was quite a full day. Most of that money would go to my mother as part of the household income.

At school I did quite well in fact. I was good at football, I was good at cricket, and I used to have the leading parts in the school plays. I can remember quite clearly my first day at school. I was sitting next to a young boy who came from Wales, and we were having a maths lesson from a very strict teacher. He was a good teacher, in fact he was the sports master as well, in charge of the football team and the cricket team, and as I became captain of both of those teams towards the end of my school life I got on very well with him. But he was a disciplinarian. The boy next to me was mucking around a little, and the teacher called him to attention and told him to put his hands upon the desk; we each had our own little desk. The boy put his hands on the desk with his knuckles upwards, and the teacher hit him across the knuckles with the thin edge of a ruler. I can tell you that it caused this lad a great deal of pain, but it also set the record straight as to what was required in this teacher's presence – that he was not prepared to have any tomfoolery and that was the sort of discipline we could expect. Remember we were all boys, we were from a tough area and we needed tough school teaching in order to keep us under control.

That man was Mr Benjamin. There was also a Mr Richards, who used to teach us in sports as well, a Mr Robinson who used to write a new school operetta every year, and Mr Jones who used to write the music for these. I can't remember the name of the PE teacher, but he was an ex regimental sergeant major. In the mornings, when the whistle blew, we had to queue up and he would take the morning exercise – jumping up and down and lifting your arms up. He was of the type that considered that sort of thing got your brain moving, a typical ex regimental sergeant major. Although he was the PE teacher, he was not involved in either the football or the cricket team, but at lunch times he held classes in the gym on how to jump over the horse and things like that. He was very keen on gymnastics which wasn't my cup of tea but lots of boys enjoyed that lunchtime experience. I used to run home at lunchtime and eat – what I used to have to eat I cannot remember but it would not have been very much – then run back and play football in the playground. Of course we didn't play with a ball, but with a block of wood which was about two or three inches square so it didn't come off the ground into the air. That was how I spent the greater portion of my lunch hour, kicking this bit of wood about. I joined the football team and then I became the captain, and from there I progressed to become a Dagenham boys player. It was a great honour at the time, particularly when you realise that there were some really famous footballers in later life who played for Dagenham boys – one of them was Mr Alf Ramsey, who you probably remember as being the manager of the English football team which won the World Cup in 1966.

I also played cricket and was captain of the cricket team, and of course on sports day I also ran and was able to keep up as well as winning some races. In my last year at school I became the headmaster's monitor, a position that in any other school would be called head boy. I was very pleased that he had chosen me to be his monitor, which meant that I had various duties to do for him, and one or two of them were a little surprising. For instance his wife was very ill in Ilford hospital and on odd occasions I had to go to Ilford hospital and take his wife a bunch of flowers, which of course the headmaster himself had paid for.

I was also a pretty good actor, and I could sing. I finished up as the lead in the last two years of the school operetta, which we used to perform in the last week before Christmas. So, as you can see, at school I played many parts and enjoyed what I was doing and I think you'll see that from the fact that in the next chapter I am going to include a personal letter from the headmaster thanking me for my work, my last exam results, and also a school report from the master who was in charge of me.

A few doors down from my house was a community centre named Kingsley Hall, run by a Sidney Russell, where I spent a great deal of my leisure time. We used to have all sorts of activities, playing table tennis, or snooker or even just meeting each other socially and having an evening of discussion. I remember quite well hearing one young girl saying to another, 'Do you know that new boy with the funny accent?' Of course they were referring to me – I had a strong Suffolk accent, although I did not realise it at the time. However the extraordinary story is that in Felixstowe I used to go to Sunday school at the Congregational Church, and every Christmas the church people used to bring presents for the deprived people of East London. A man in his car used to come to the church to collect these presents, and it was no other than Sidney Russell who used to take them back to Kingsley Hall. What a story, however the final twist is that Max Wotton, who was a superintendent of the Sunday school in Felixstowe at that time, was the best man at my wedding.

Talking of Christmas, I have to say that during the whole of my childhood

I cannot remember Christmas ever playing a large part in my life. Firstly at Felixstowe I can never remember a Christmas tree or putting up decorations or having a special meal for Christmas lunch. I know that I did not expect very much. It was always just one present in a stocking at the bottom of my bed, it could be a box of dominoes or a snakes and ladders game, or once I remember it was a torch. There would be an apple and an orange and some sweets, and that was the extent of my presents. When I came to Dagenham things were even worse than they were in Felixstowe. Although I use the word 'worse', I didn't feel deprived, although I did realise that perhaps there were other children who treated Christmas as a special part of the year, whereas to me it was simply another day. Poverty in those days was when there was no money in the house and very little food on the table.

One particular Christmas in Dagenham, I can't remember exactly how old I was, but I know that there was no money, no money whatsoever. At the time we were living off benefit vouchers that we used to spend at the grocery store in order to keep going. I didn't expect very much and of course, I didn't get very much, but it didn't matter. I can remember one terrible thing at that particular time. I'll tell you about it because it did happen to me and it had a great effect on me at the time. I came down and found that my mother had just put her head in the gas oven with the gas full on and was attempting to commit suicide. Things had got to her. Dan and I found her. She had not been ill but of course her mental state was obviously at its very lowest point.

Now look at what young children expect with regard to Christmas and the number of presents they have, all displayed around a Christmas tree, and the great excitement there is on Christmas morning of opening presents. I have often wondered, when I have been a part of that particular ceremony, whether those opening the presents, particularly the younger ones, are in fact any happier in their lives than I was as a child with, as I've explained, very little. I'm not sure whether we've gone a little bit too far. I hope I have not been talking as though I was the only child in the world who had a poor Christmas day. There were many children who were in the same position as I was, and of course when you think worldwide, those poor children who are born in unfortunate circumstances in other parts of the world – their lives are an absolute misery. I can only say that my childhood had some very happy memories indeed.

In 1936 I had to miss the school examinations because my mother kept me home to look after Doreen, who was a baby at the time. I cannot tell you what I actually did, other than I was home and I was, I guess, talking to her. She was very ill. What her complaint was I have absolutely no idea, but I'd say that young babies, from time to time, do get these sort of illnesses which are difficult. In any case, I'm not sure who was looking after her medical condition, or not, all I know is that I was at home looking after her. My mother was in no sort of mental state, she was struggling, as we all were, and so I stayed at home during that period. A fondness was formed between Doreen and me, and from time to time Doreen refers to it; she obviously remembers it a great deal more than I do, but never the less a bond was formed then and has continued over the years. We have very often talked about the time that she was an ill baby and I, being somebody of twelve years or so, had to look after her. It's a strange thing I guess because throughout the whole of my life I seem to have liked babies. I always talk to them, I like seeing them in prams and asking how old they are and have always been interested in babies and little children.

The situation between my mother and my stepfather was, to say the least, somewhat strange. My grandmother was a formidable person and so was my mother, a very formidable person. In later years, when she became a grandmother, she came to be known as Granny Murray, and when the family got together we'd always talk about Granny Murray and how she acted as a person through the whole of our lives. She was the boss. Dan, a very quiet man, could be sitting in a room and you wouldn't really realise that he was there – he didn't really have many conversations with anyone. I can't say that he ever acted as a father towards me, but on the other hand he never did anything detrimental. If my mother wanted things done she would certainly tell Dan – this needs decorating, or some job needs doing, do the washing up, things like that. She had her own way of doing things, and if you didn't do those things in her way, she was quick to instruct you. She was the only one who was allowed to put coal on the fire because anybody else doing it would make too much dust. If you were to make a cup of tea, you weren't allowed to pour it out because you would be likely to spill some onto the tea cloth. She even had her own way of wrapping up stuff that was going to be put in the dustbin. You wrapped it up in newspaper, and she very often used to get quite uptight about 'You don't wrap it that way, you wrap it this way.' The house was absolutely spick and span, she was a stickler for tidiness and cleanliness, and you could have eaten off the kitchen floor, let alone the dining table. She was always polishing this, or cleaning this, or washing this or that, she was a stickler for things being absolutely right. I suppose she was, pure and simply, house-proud. The story of the curtains I will tell you later on; it's always been a tale which has made people laugh, because the curtains were not allowed to be touched by anybody other than herself – she knew each crease, and the exact position that a curtain should be in.

My mother was the sort of person, I'm afraid, who always had to be right.

During the war when rationing came along, and whenever there were supplies in the shops, there were always queues, and if you tried to push in front of her you were in very serious trouble. Her views of life were extremely left wing and in later life she and I clashed over politics. During election times after the war her house was the committee rooms for the communist party, in order to organise people to go to the polls.

Before I leave my school days, I will have to tell you this little story. I had been selected to play for the Dagenham boys, and I was extremely pleased that I had been selected a year earlier than most boys would have had the chance. Mr Richards, who was in charge of the school football team along with Mr Benjamin, could see that I was used to playing in a pair of very old, scrappy football boots, I have no idea how I came across them and they were certainly well beyond the stage where you could really call them football boots. Mr Richards took me to his house, where I met his wife and his two small children, and he gave me a pair of football boots with the shin pads and the socks. He told me that he no longer had a use for them and he hoped that I was happy to have them, which I certainly was, and of course I used those boots all the time I was playing schoolboy football. What a gesture, what a man. I shall never forget his name or his kindness.

I would like to show you a photograph of my mother and her neighbour Mrs Tuckfield. They were very close friends and neighbours during those 1930s years; my mother is the one with the carpet slippers on. Both of these ladies were in their mid-thirties and you can see just what a toll it had taken on them, bringing up a family and putting food on the table, clothes on their backs, paying the rent, heating the house during the winter time, sometimes with almost nothing in the house and very little money to spend. All I can say is that, in Dagenham, we were not the only families like that; 80–90% of families all over the country in those years of Depression in the 1930s had to struggle, day by day, week by week to survive. I think perhaps it made us the people that we are today, and it has certainly had repercussions on me for many of the actions which I have taken later on in life.

You have to remember that people were not just neighbours in those days, they were also friends, and a very strong bond grew between people who lived a few doors or so from each other. Nobody was any different from anybody else, nobody was superior. They were all in this Depression together and trying to live as happy a life as they possibly could under some rather severe circumstances. A friend of my mother's lived some four or five doors away. I used to have to call on her on a Monday evening before I did my paper round. I took her son's suit to the pawn brokers, who offered money for the suit, which I used to take back to her. I have no idea how

Mum and Mrs Tuckfield. The Parsloe Belles

much money was involved but in those days we talked about pence and pennies. Something that cost a shilling was expensive. Certainly, something that cost a pound would have been far out of the reach of ordinary folk. However, after school on a Friday I used to have to collect the money that she had got together to redeem her son's suit and I used to go to the pawn broker, pay the money over and pick up the suit. He obviously wanted it for the weekends, but during the week it was in the pawn broker's shop, and that was one way in which he would live throughout the week. I have no doubt that her son paid her some money over on the Friday, for his keep, and that's how she redeemed the suit for him to wear at the weekends. There are many stories like that that can be told. It was of no significance that people went to pawn brokers and such like in order to survive from one week to another.

3

The time came for me to leave school, you were only at school until you were fourteen, and as I was getting close to fourteen I actually left school then. I had no qualifications, of course we didn't take any outside exams, and so I was left with just these two reports, and I'll note them down because I have been extremely proud of my last school reports that I got from Halbett Street. The first reference is actually from the headmaster, and it says this:

> John Skelton has attended this school since 1935 and is leaving today. Throughout this period his conduct, attendance and work has been excellent. He has always occupied a high position in the top class. An excellent footballer, a keen actor and also took part in all the activities of school life. He has been most helpful and has carried out many duties outside his ordinary schoolwork, and in every way I have found him hardworking, honest and thoroughly reliable. I have no reservation to make in giving him the strongest possible recommendation.
>
> J. S. Scougall, Headmaster

The other report, which is the school report that people got when they left school, came from my house master: 'Age leaving: fourteen. Date of leaving: 13th of the 4th 1937. Period at this school: three years, application was science and his best subjects were science and mathematics.' The general remarks were as follows: 'A very fine type of boy, who has done very well in school. Has also excellently been the school captain in cricket and football. In school operetta he has proven himself, a very good actor.' Then there was a little note written by the headmaster, Mr Scougall, which said, 'This boy is reliable in every way.'

I have now checked on the actual date on which I left school by looking at my full school reports which I had each year. It was definitely January 1938 and not 1937 as the house master had it, and surprisingly enough it was the date of the letter which the Headmaster had put as well. I think because it was January they had not yet changed from '37 to '38. As you can see from that date, I left school before I was fourteen – I was not fourteen until 22 April 1938, but it didn't mean that I couldn't go forward and get into employment. it was just simply the case that when you left school, you tried to get yourself employment and that's what I started to do.

Now I had to start looking for a job at not quite fourteen. I'm absolutely useless as a DIY person, my hands were never meant to muck about with cars or motorbikes, or anything of a technical nature, and that has been the case throughout my whole life. However, I was very good with writing, I was very neat with arithmetic, and so working in an office was obviously the career path that I should follow. How was I going to go about this? First of all, somehow or another I had to get a suit. I certainly couldn't go for an interview for an office job without having a decent suit and a shirt.

Of course my clothes were not something which I was ashamed to be wearing because everybody was the same, but if I was going to London, which is where I wanted to get to and work, somehow or another I'd have to get a suit. In those days Burtons were the people who advertised their suits, off the hook, for two pounds ten shillings, a lot of money. But of course there was a possibility of hire purchase or HP. There was a Burtons pretty close to where we lived, so that's where I went to have a look to purchase my first suit. Now of course came the question of how much a week it was going to cost or the length of HP I was going to have. I have no idea now how much that suit cost but I know my mother said that the money I used to earn from my paper rounds could pay at least the first week or two of instalments, until I'd been paid from getting a job. She had to come into the tailors, to Burtons, to sign the agreement. I bought a shirt, a tie, and the suit. I came home and I felt like the king of the castle.

Now I had to get to the labour exchange to find out where employment was available. They sent me to the labour exchange in Liverpool Street. Of course I lived in Dagenham, and I had to go and have this interview in the labour exchange in Liverpool Street – another few shillings extra that I had to find for the fare to London. But I was armed with my suit, my shirt, and my tie, and I felt a million dollars because in my pocket, of course, was the letter I'd got from the headmaster of the school and my school reports. I also had some of the work I had done when I was only around seven or eight years old, which was extremely neat and tidy. I got the job.

I started work for a company called Gallenkamp and Co, who dealt with medical supplies of all sorts to hospitals and doctors' surgeries, etc. It was in Sun Street, EC1, that's where I became their office boy – my wages were twelve shillings and six pence per week. Of course everybody was paid weekly in those days, and my main problem was that I had to have a season ticket in order to travel backwards and forwards from Dagenham to Moorgate station. I've no recollection of how I financed the first week's train fares, but somehow or another I overcame this. That's how I started as the office boy there and went backwards and forwards every day. I'm not sure how much money I gave my mother and how much I kept for myself but you can be sure that I always had the family in my mind. I was not the sort of person who would say, 'Well look, I've earned it and it's all mine.'

I now started to become more of an adult, mixing in London and at the same time talking to people on the trains etc., I got a different perspective in life. My main activities outside work were at Kingsley Hall and there was plenty that used to go on there in the way of table tennis and snooker. Of course we did have some Saturday night dances, at which I was not very proficient, and so I decided I would go to a dance class. It was held on a Wednesday in a small hall very close to where I lived, and the class was sixpence per session. I thoroughly enjoyed it and became, although I say it myself, a very good ballroom dancer; in fact I won a couple of certificates for being one of the best of the young ballroom dancers. So then when I went to Kingsley Hall on a Saturday for their dances I was quite able to do whatever dance was called.

Very often on a Saturday night, instead of going to Kingsley Hall, we youngsters would go to a very posh dance hotel which held evening dances. Remember that I was only around fourteen, maybe just fifteen, but I knew I could dance. Remember too that in those days girls often didn't dance with each other. They had to wait until such time that a male asked them to dance before they got on the floor, and of course those who were left out time and time again were known as wallflowers. We males were looking for, not necessarily the best looking, but certainly the person who could dance the best. We were interested only in whether she could dance or whether she couldn't dance, there was no question of, say, having a girlfriend to take out to the cinema and that, because one didn't earn sufficient money. In any case, in my position, quite a bit of money went to my mother to help with the family and rent, and so the question of asking a girl if she would like a drink never arose, and when you were dancing the last waltz you didn't think of seeing somebody home. It was one of those things, you went to the dance, you did your dancing and you came away.

Those girls who weren't asked for a dance were a bit unfortunate, but there used to be one particular dance called the 'ladies excuse me'. That meant that the ladies could go onto the dance floor, pick a partner they wanted to dance with, tap on their arm and say 'Excuse me, please', a request that could not be refused. So they got dances that way. It was a bit of a nuisance if you were dancing with someone who was a good dancer and someone came along and excused you, and then you found that you were dancing with somebody who'd got two left feet. That was an unfortunate situation but there it is; that was all in the game.

Another way in which girls got partners was that the girls would make a circle facing outwards, and the men would make an outer circle facing inwards. The girls walked one way and the males walked the other way. When the music stopped you danced with the person who was in front of you. I did not have a girlfriend as such, I was quite happy to carry on doing exactly what I was doing with my activities at Kingsley Hall and dancing my way around the dance floor on a Saturday night.

However, because I was employed in London we had to work on Saturday mornings as well. I started to support the Arsenal because I was close to Finsbury Park station, and I could get there quite easily from where I worked in Sun Street. So I started to support Arsenal on a Saturday afternoon and got to know the team very well. I have supported them ever since – Arsenal have always been my team and I can go back to the days of Herbert Chapman and the way in which Arsenal were considered to be one of the very top teams in England at the time.

After I'd been working at Gallenkamps for some four or five months I noticed that quite a lot of the people who worked there actually travelled by bicycle to work, as opposed to paying for either bus fares or train fares. I was only earning twelve and sixpence per week and my monthly season ticket was ten shillings a month, so two and six had to be saved for the monthly season ticket. I thought that what I would do was cycle. Of course I hadn't got a bicycle so it meant another hire purchase agreement, with the ten shillings a month going towards the cost of the cycle. I can't remember now exactly how much I saved by going by bike instead of by bus or train, but I do know that I've always been the sort of person who looks at money fairly closely and decides that spending money when its unnecessary is the sort of thing that should never be part of my life.

So there I was, a cyclist, and I was travelling from Dagenham to Sun Street – the mileage is lost to me, I've no idea. I think it used to take me about an hour to cycle. I used to go along the Barking bypass then along Whitechapel Road, right into Liverpool Street. Of course it meant I had to have a cape for the rainy weather, and I used to cycle in an old pair of trousers and carry my suit trousers in a bag, so that if it did rain they didn't get wet and certainly didn't get too shiny in the pants. Sometimes conditions were not too good, particularly on the foggy days, but as far as I was concerned it meant that I was a little bit better off financially doing that than giving money to the rail company for the monthly season ticket.

Towards the end of 1938 I was promoted and instead of being the office boy I was put into the advertising department. I worked with the advertising manager and I was given a three shillings a week increase, which made my money fifteen shillings and sixpence a week. I thought at the time that I was very rich because I didn't spend too much. I was a non-smoker, whenever I went out to Kingsley Hall that was a non-alcoholic place, and when I went out dancing elsewhere I had two half pints of beer, that was as much as I was going to have. So I felt that I was quite comfortable at that time.

Unfortunately of course, the war was now being spoken about a great deal and the name of Adolf Hitler who was at that time thinking in terms of overrunning Europe and taking over the whole of Europe by force. He was building up a tremendous air force and a large army; his sights were definitely on Europe and taking over the whole lot. My mother was terrified. I couldn't understand why because she was a formidable person but the war was one of the thing that she really could not really take, that is for sure, and she often spoke about it in terms of 'I wonder what exactly would happen ...' Of course it was in late 1938 that Neville Chamberlain, who was the Prime Minister at that time, went to Germany while Adolf Hitler was growing in power and came back waving this piece of paper and saying that it was peace in our time. Chamberlain said that he had secured a deal with Adolf Hitler, that Hitler had no commitments at all to over-run Europe and certainly not to over-run us. Unfortunately all that turned out to be a myth because in the beginning of 1939, or just after, Hitler started again, taking bits and pieces from Europe and over-running country after country.

In 1939 we were all issued with a gas mask and the fact that Neville Chamberlain had this piece of paper was absolutely of no concern whatsoever. We had to go and queue up and be issued with the gas masks and there was obviously war being talked about day by day. Towards the middle of September they even issued us with parts of an air raid shelter to dig into each garden. The lorries came along, they'd throw the parts off onto the pavement and we then had to go and pick up those bits of corrugated iron, dig a massive hole in the back garden, plant the corrugated iron in that hole, put the roof on and cover it back up with the dirt we had dug out before. People talked about air raids and we had our air raid shelter already dug into the garden. It was a very tense time; nobody knew exactly what was going to happen.

I was still working in London and still enjoying my dancing and my activities at Kingsley Hall. Fortunately for me I appeared to be quite a popular person because I could sing, dance and apparently had the ability to make people laugh for some reason or another. I didn't tell jokes but I fitted in to people's conversations and before you knew it people were laughing. It wasn't a very serious time for me in as much as I always thought that even if a war started, sometime or another, I would end up in the midst of it and everything would turn out to be OK. Luckily for me I did come through the war, but that is another story to be told a little later.

4

On the day war was declared, which was 3 September 1939 at eleven o'clock, I was actually in London with Gallenkamps. We were filling sand bags and putting the sand bags around the building hoping they would help to deflect any sort of blast that would come from bombs being dropped. Because we all anticipated that the moment war was declared, bombs would be dropped. At eleven o'clock that day, Neville Chamberlain came on the radio and said that we were now at war with Germany. Adolf Hitler had assured him (on that little piece of paper that he'd waved about) that he had no further ideas to over-run Europe, but he actually invaded Poland and of course that was the last straw.

Almost immediately, a few minutes after Chamberlain's speech, a siren went off indicating that an air raid was imminent and that we should go to our air raid shelters. People were white faced, not knowing quite what was going to happen as it was a new experience for everybody. Some few minutes later, it seemed a lifetime really, another siren went off to say that it was all clear; it was all a mistake. We ourselves had gone down into the shelter which was provided by Gallenkamps and we were grim faced. People looked at each other and wondered when the end was going to come. That didn't happen, so I just went home. My mother was in a terrible state and it wasn't long, only a matter of days really, before she decided that she didn't want to stay in Dagenham, which was close to London where we knew that bombs would be falling. So she moved; she went from Dagenham to a place called Arbourfield which was pretty close to Reading. My step-father Dan had a friend he was working with, who was able to look after my mother and two children, and of course Dan himself.

My mother and Dan took Brian and Doreen with them and I was left. I moved in with the people next door as a lodger. My sister Gladys moved into the East End with her then boyfriend and his mother and brother, and that was the outcome of what happened to us in those first weeks of the war.

You must remember that on 3 September 1939, from the moment that war was declared, everyone's lives changed; it was never going to be the same again. It affected everybody in every way possible. There was wholesale evacuation of children from the cities where they expected the greater proportion of the bombing. These children were taken away by rail and I'm sure you will have seen photographs of these large parties of children with their parents saying goodbye to them, with their gas masks hung round their necks and their badges with their names and addresses on and where they were going. Nobody knew where they were going, nobody was told exactly where they would end up and whose family they would end up with. Of course what happened was that some children ended up in very nice accommodation whereas others were somewhat unlucky, ending up in places where the people were not very nice to them. If you want to read more about evacuees, I would recommend that you go to the British War Museum in London, where there is a whole section on the evacuation. There are letters from children that are absolutely heartbreaking, in as much that the children were so unhappy and wanted to come home, whereas other children were very happy indeed and settled in to a different life altogether. They were safe of course, at least that was the idea of it. The parents were not happy; imagine sending your children away to save them but having to stay put yourself hoping for the best.

What was happening outside was that we were building up our forces, factories were mainly for ammunition, aircrafts, ships etc. Then conscription was brought in for anyone who reached the age of eighteen to go into the army, the navy or the air force. You didn't have a choice, you had to go into whatever force they put you into. As the war went on, eighteen then became nineteen and twenty and twenty-one, it didn't stop just there.

Another thing, rationing, was very quickly introduced for almost everything you could think of. We were a country that relied for our standard of living on imports which had to be brought in by sea, which was no longer a safe place. Ships were mainly used in a convoy method to bring in supplies where necessary. A small item illustrates the difficulties: there were no bananas brought into this country during the war. Children didn't know what a banana tasted or looked like. Of course other types of fruit we were able to grow in our own orchards.

Our forces were being mobilised and the army was sent to France. It was called the BEF, the British Expeditionary Force, and for them certainly when they went no one quite knew what was going to happen. By Christmas time 1939, and into 1940, the whole thing was talked about as though it was a 'phoney war'; that is, that nothing seemed to happen. Of course we had rationing, and the blackout. All houses had to have blinds so that light didn't shine out into the street, so everywhere was in darkness. The only indication that there was something different really at that particular time was the fact that the forces were being sent to France, as I've said. So my mother came back. I think she was away for some three or four months, not much longer than that, then she came back and of course I moved in with her as opposed to lodging next door, but my sister didn't. She stayed with her boyfriend and his mother. She never actually came back home again.

So things just trundled along until Germany over ran Belgium, France, Holland. France gave in very quickly and our forces, the British Expeditionary Force, were slowly but surely forced back, beaten really, by the mighty German army. Of course you all remember the story of the people, British and French soldiers, who were saved by the small boats who got together and the evacuation from Dunkirk. That part of history I'm sure I don't need to repeat. Two hundred and fifty thousand or so troops were saved and came back to this country via these little ships, they were bombarded all the way back, ships mustered from various parts of the south coast. We were now alone in this country waiting for what everyone expected was going to be an onslaught by Adolf Hitler after which we would have been part of his empire. My mother, with tears in her eyes, said, 'Germany have beaten us, it's all over. What will happen to us?' She walked around mumbling 'What is going to happen to us?', over and over again. This was how thousands of people were feeling and only those of us living at that time can understand how morale had sank to such a very low level.

Then Winston Churchill gave his famous speech to the House of Commons and was broadcast to the nation. This is what he said: 'We shall go on to the end. We shall fight in France, we shall fight in the seas and oceans, we shall fight with growing confidence and growing strength in the air, we shall defend our island whatever the cost may be. We shall fight on the beaches, we shall fight on the landing grounds, we shall fight in the fields and in the streets, we shall fight in the hills; we shall never surrender.' The mood of the nation changed. There was an uplift in spirits which had not been felt previously, all from the power of Sir Winston's oration. I cannot put into words the difference that people were feeling after they heard that speech.

It was during the 1940s, I remember it very clearly, there had been no attempt to invade us but the Blitz started. The first attack on London was on 7 September 1940. I was walking down the road with my friends and the sirens went off. Unfortunately we thought, 'Oh well this is another one of those mistakes,' but it wasn't. There were hundreds, well it looked like hundreds, of bombers in the sky, we could see them coming over towards London, and then we saw the fires. It was the first Blitz; it was the first raid that happened in London. I went home, we went down into our shelter and looked at each other, and we thought, 'Well, this really is the beginning of the end.'

I need to go back a little bit now, because what I'm going to tell you happened before the Blitz started. I was reading the newspaper and I saw an advert for an office boy at William Warne & Co Ltd, who were rubber manufacturers in Barking. Now Barking was not a stone's throw from Dagenham and that meant I would only have a short cycle ride to get there. Not only that, the job was being advertised as a weekly wage of one pound and one shilling. I thought, 'My God, if I could get that job I would not quite know what to do with that extra money.' I wrote away for the job, I had an interview, and I got the job. The strange thing was that when I arrived on the first day there was another boy who was taken on at the same time – apparently there were always two office boys in this office, in the accounts department, and we were both starting on the same day. His name was John Reese. We became friends then and we remained friends right up until his death a few years ago. I'll tell you a little bit more about that later on.

The man who was in charge of the office there said, 'Well, which one is to be the number one office boy? What has the secretary told you you were to be?' We said, 'No, we've both come but we don't know.' Well the only difference between being the number one office boy and the number two office boy was that the number one office boy filed the yellow copies and the number two office boy filed the white copies. We tossed a coin. I lost. John Reese won and so he used to file the yellows and I used to file the whites. Of course we did have to do quite a lot of other things, we were writing amounts of money into books, and so on. It was quite an interesting job and it was there that I met Peggy Goater. She was later to become Peggy Skelton, but I'll tell you a little bit more about that in time.

I enjoyed working in Barking. I didn't have to travel that far and John Reese and I got on quite well, we were good friends. We were about the same age and had the same interests. In fact from time to time we played football together in the same team. The young lady I've mentioned, Peggy Goater, she was a comptometer operator. Comptometers were the fore-runners of computers, much ahead of calculators and you had to be pretty good at arithmetic etc. to operate them. In order to become a comptometer operator Peggy had to go to a particular comptometer school for some three months and pay privately to have lessons to become a fully fledged comptometer operator. At the end of the comptometer course one student was awarded the Felt & Tarrent Ring, given to the student who had per-formed best through the whole of the course. Peggy got this ring. It was called the Felt & Tarrent ring because Felt & Tarrent were the comptometer manufacturers and they also ran the courses. I can tell you that she was mighty proud of this ring and she wore it for years and years. In fact the Felt & Tarrent ring is still in the family. Back then Peggy used to come into our office, not very often because she was in another office with two other comptometer operators. She did tell me very much later that she used to like taking my books, as opposed to the other John's books, because mine were much neater than his. I didn't know that at the time – it was a secret that she told me later on in life.

Then the Blitz came, night after night after night, as you will know. It lasted until the following May. William Warne & Co decided they'd had enough of the constant Blitz and of course were worried about the factory being in Barking, which was closer to London than Dagenham. They decided that some twenty-five people from the accounts department and one or two other people would be evacuated to the Managing Director's house in a place near Brentwood, just outside Warley. It was a very big house and they had turned it into offices. We went there on Mondays and worked there from Monday to Friday, all the week, and all the accounts, records, etc. were housed there. The business of the accounts department was run from Warley as opposed to being in Barking. The name of the house was Warley Lea.

This meant of course that people became very close to each other and we became attached to the whole group. After work there was the evening to get through and of course we sat and had our meals in the house. Warley Lea was the sort of house that had an annex which had been servants' quarters and such. It was a very large house indeed and there was a dormitory for the male section as well as one for the female section, and people got on very well with each other. Now Peggy Goater was one of those people who came from the other side of the tracks to me. She was an only child, she lived in a private house in East Ham and she was some two years older than me. Before the war she had trained, or was training, to be a classical concert pianist – by the time she was sixteen or seventeen she was playing solo at East Ham town hall in front of large audiences with an orchestra behind her. She was very close to her mother. Sadly her mother and father had lost two other children, one called Hazel and one called Donald, at thirteen months and just a few months old. So Peggy was an only child who was cossetted. She couldn't go out anywhere, she was never allowed out in the street, she was never allowed to go to anybody else's house in case she caught some germs or something. She had one friend who would come to her house. She used to go to church, she was a Methodist and she used to go to the chapel three times on a Sunday and take the choirs so she could play the organ, she did this quite often. Her father was foreman maintenance fitter on night shifts and so she became very attached to her mother and her mother became very attached to her. Peggy was a quiet soul who really knew very

27

little about the outside world and when she came to Warley she saw a different life. She saw that there was a life which she rather liked, and the business of people getting together, and going out together, and laughing and talking really was an eye opener to her.

Warley Lea and the large garden

Peggy was finding a life totally different from the life she had been leading up until then. She was eighteen and I was sixteen. Unfortunately in the early days she went home and told her mother that there was one horrible boy there, John Skelton, who was always first for everything. He took the best bacon at breakfast time and he was one of those people who she didn't really like at all, and she told her mother so, which was a bit unfortunate for me. However, later on in life her mother asked, 'Well what changed?' and Peggy said, 'He was always jack the lad, he made me laugh. Not only that he was a great dancer and I was desperate, absolutely desperate to learn to dance and could not dance a step.'

And so a relationship started to be formed. We would hold dances, and we would play table tennis and all other sorts of activities, but Peggy loved to dance. She wanted to dance but couldn't dance a step, and I was the one who was going to teach her. Well, as you know, with ballroom dancing what happens is you get hold of your partner and you become very close to each other, and from that moment really, after a short time of course, there was always the squeezing of the hand or a kiss on the cheek and everything progressed from there. We became extremely attached to each other, so much so that although at first we used to go home on Friday night to come back and start work on Monday, a lot of us teenagers or slightly older started to come back on Sunday night for a bit of a hoo-ha. Of course we didn't get any breakfast on the Monday morning, so Peggy decided that she'd got to tell her mother that she enjoyed things so much that, instead of going back to work on Monday, she was going to go back on Sunday afternoon. I'm sure this caused eruptions in their house but in the end she got her way. A relationship grew, but when I say relationship, I pure and simply mean that we were boyfriend and girlfriend, and that's where it began and ended.

We spent time together, we went to the cinema together. This story goes around my family which is quite right: Peggy had a very sweet tooth and liked nothing more than meringues or any cake of any sweet nature. Before we went into the cinema with my friend John Reese and his girlfriend, we might have a cup of tea and Peggy would definitely have a meringue. Unfortunately in those days we didn't have too much money. I used to offer her another meringue, and if she had the second meringue then I didn't have enough money for us to come back on the bus and we would have to walk. With bated breath we waited to see if she would have the second one, and more often than not we ended up walking. And so we walked back from Brentwood to Warley – two, three, four miles I can't quite remember. It's a story that goes round our family time and time again, how Dad used to have to walk back because Mummie had the second meringue.

There came the time when Peggy had to go home to her mother and tell her that that horrible boy she first knew when she went to Warley had now become her boyfriend, and so we were boyfriend and girlfriend. I can well imagine what her mother said, knowing her as I do now as opposed to then.

This went on for some six or seven months, but the Blitz eventually ended and it was decided that we should go back to Barking. But unfortunately just previous to us going back a bomb had dropped in East Ham where Peggy lived, and damaged their house in Mitcham Road. Although it was habitable, it had had considerable damage done to windows and so on. That had frightened Peggy's mother and father and so they moved away. They made this move because Peggy's mothers' family offered accommodation to them in Hemel Hempstead. So Peggy never went back to William Warne & Co in Barking, she moved out to Hemel Hempstead and I of course was still living in Dagenham.

This made life difficult for us. Peggy got a job working in St Pancras town hall in Euston, London, and travelled up by train from Hemel to Euston every day so there were difficulties now with us keeping in touch. We didn't have telephones and there was no way of communicating other than writing to each other and fixing up times when we would meet. It would sometimes be in London just after she had left work, although I also used to go into the town hall. I got quite friendly with a number of her working partners. Or there were times when I went to Hemel and stayed the weekend with the people who lived next door to Peggy's mother and father. And so we did keep in touch with each other in that way – it was a relationship which was a little bit difficult, but I can tell you that it didn't make any difference to how we felt about each other. I'm sure that she knew at that very early stage that I was the right person for her, and I certainly knew that she was the right person for me. Then I turned seventeen and of course, at eighteen I was going to be called up. I made the decision that I wanted to go into the Royal Navy as opposed to the army or air force, and so I invented the fact that instead of being born in 1924 I had arrived in 1923. That meant I was eighteen and I was going to join the navy.

So I went and enrolled, in Romford I think, where I had the medical and of course in those days, they didn't test your eyes they just counted them. If you'd got two eyes you were fit, there was no question of real medical examination. Certainly they didn't look at birth certificates or anything like that. I was accepted and I just waited for my letter to come to say where I had to report to.

While I was at Warley Lea my brothers Brian and Bobby were evacuated to Cornwall with the school. They lived with two people by the name of Mr and Mrs Lilly, who were very kind to both Brian and Bobby – in fact, they treated them like their own children. They had no children of their own and the two boys came to their house. The living conditions were somewhat primitive; an outside toilet at the bottom of the garden, the lighting and getting of water, etc. It was in Penryn or just outside Penryn, and was a very old-fashioned situation but they were well loved. Both Brian and Bobby were there for some four years, and they loved every moment of the life that they had down there in Cornwall. Bobby came back when he was fourteen, because he was going to start work and of course there was not too much work to be had in a small Cornish village, but his mind was always that he would go back to Cornwall to live at some time and when he retired at sixty-five, that's exactly what he did. He went back to live in a bungalow which he and his wife built themselves in Penryn, not a stone's throw from where he was evacuated. He just loved Cornwall and he's extremely happy in his retirement there.

I was now waiting for my papers to arrive to tell me where I had to report to and when. They came through and I had to report to HMS *Collinwood*, which is just outside Portsmouth, on 16 December 1941. I would be missing Christmas of course but Christmas was never a day that was very special to me. So I now had to prepare to go into the Navy and that's where the next part of my book really begins: going to HMS *Collinwood*, doing my training, then finishing the training and being posted, my first post actually being a secret radar station in the northern part of Iceland. I'll tell you more about that as the book goes on.

5

At HMS *Collinwood* we were quickly examined and given our uniforms which included underwear etc. We then had to stamp our own name on each item with a block which was provided for us. We were paid one shilling per week, with my mother getting an allowance of some shillings per week – you have to remember that everything was provided. We were not allowed out of the premises for six weeks and were rationed to one letter per week.

It was a very harsh winter and standing on the parade grounds every morning with just a naval uniform on was no joke, although I quickly caught on to the instructions 'Fall out RCs' and men ran from the ranks to the gym which was warm and cosy. I wondered what it meant, RC, then I realised we were having a church service and so RC meant Roman Catholic. I quickly became an RC. I think the experience that sticks in my mind more than anything else was a day we had our rowing instructions. Down to old Portsmouth we went in almost a blizzard with just our uniform on and had to row to the end of the harbour and back. I can assure you that I have never felt so down and wretched in my life, even my mother would have cried for me.

The course was twelve weeks and then I went into Portsmouth barracks and had a seven-day leave. I will include a photograph of my class mates, but I'm ashamed to say that I could not name a single one, and I do not know how many of them survived the war. Some would certainly be dead; one was a teacher of thirty years of age conscripted into the navy. You see, he was not in a reserved occupation. What started off as people of eighteen being conscripted in the very early part of the war, turned into bigger rows and rows and rows of conscripts. I can't tell you what the maximum age was at which you were able to feel that you were not going to be called up into one of the fighting forces.

And so I was now on my way to a seven-day leave. It did mean that I became more involved with Peggy's mother and father, so I must backtrack a little and tell you more of the difference between Peggy's circumstances and upbringing, and mine. As you'll recall I really had very little, coming from an extremely poor council house background, being one of seven children, but I was never backward about coming forward. I knew that I had something. Although I say it myself, people seemed to like me and liked to

My class at Collinwood. I am second from right on second row from back

be in my company. I suppose you could say I had more confidence than ability. Peggy, on the other hand, came from a private house, her father was a night foreman, obviously working full time nights but it meant that he earned over the average wage for those days. However he was not in charge; Peggy's mother was, Peggy's mother was a very good dressmaker and so you could be sure that Peggy was always well dressed. She and her mother attended chapel three times on a Sunday, and of course it meant a different hat, coat, etc. for the morning and evening services they attended. Peggy was also the stand-in organist when necessary, and of course before the war Peggy did her studies on the piano for some six hours per day, she didn't actually go to work after she left school. Her father was prone to rage attacks; I suppose you would say today that he had PTSD from the First World War, where he spent long periods in the front line trenches in France. I really saw little of him and when I did we got on very well. However I was not popular with Peggy's mother. She realised that when Peggy went to Warley Lea with the company that we worked for, she had lost control of Peggy, and she had come back a very different person. Peggy did indeed see a different side to life and she very much liked what she saw, and as far as her mother was concerned I was the one responsible for that.

However the seven days' leave arrived. Of course, I would spend some time with my mother but most would be spent with Peggy and her mother.

During the period when I had been away Peggy had moved with her mother and father from the lodgings they had to a private rented bungalow on a very nice estate at Highridge Road, still in Hemel Hempstead of course. Highridge Road was where I was going to stay on my first leave, and in fact is where I lived when the war was over and I came back to civilian life. When it came to the end of the leave Peggy and I both realised just how much we really loved each other, but there was the uncertainty of the future. I was going back to be sent somewhere or other, and neither of us knew if we'd see each other again. I remember the words she said when I left, although she did not come to the station: 'Please come back to me, safe and sound.' Some tears fell, and I was away.

When I arrived back at HMS *Victory*, which was Portsmouth barracks, I went on a six-week course to become a radar operator, and then I was part of a fairly new division of the Navy. After the course, in fact two days after I finished, I was drafted to what was to be known as HMS *Baldur*. I was extremely unfortunate because there were fourteen other people in this draft and they had all come back from a special ten days' leave, because of the nature of the draft. I lost out because I was taking the place of someone who did not return from their leave. I was told that all future letters to me should be addressed to HMS *Baldur*. I was not happy with the circumstances as we were issued with special arctic clothing, measured for a set of skis and had snow shoes; there was mystery after mystery. We were soon heading for the troop ship in Greenock, which was to take us over to Reykjavik, the capital of Iceland. The United States of America, when they came into the war, invaded Iceland and they took over that country. I'm sure that the name of the troop ship was *Orduna*, and there were about 3000 soldiers, airmen, etc., aboard a vessel which was really only meant to carry say about 1000. It was chaos. More so when we went through some very rough seas and practically all of those aboard were being violently sea sick, myself included. I don't know if you've ever been sea sick, but you get to the stage where death would be better than living. Bodies were lying prostrate on top deck, with vomit and sea washing over them every few minutes – you would have to have seen it to really visualise the scene. One of the big problems of the war was how to transport troops who would be fit to fight when they arrived, and that problem was never solved.

Arriving in Reykjavik we transferred to a small ship which was going to take our boxes of equipment and ourselves to the final destination, Saebol in the northern tip of Iceland. While we were on board we were told what the assignment really was. We would be in this extreme isolated spot where there were only three houses, to be called the Admiralty secret experimental station Saebol, where we would set up a radar site on top of the mountain to track shipping. We talked of Reykjavik, as it was known that the German battle ships were in that area looking out for convoys which were passing by on their way to Murmansk, in Russia, with military equipment for Russia.

The marines had been there before us, in fact the summer before us, and had built special mission huts, put a railway into the top of the mountain, and also put a gun ring on the top of the mountain which would home our radar set with the gun room moving the aerial around. What we brought with us was the radar equipment, which we had portered ashore, along with other necessary equipment. We were helped by some of the local Icelanders who lived on the three farms. This was to be my home for the next thirteen months. It was the end of March 1942, so it would to be April 1943 before I saw civilisation again. There was no naval discipline, no naval uniform; everyone was called by their Christian names. We each had a pair of skis, a rifle and arctic clothing. The rifle was because of the fear of a German submarine coming in and wiping us out, as they did many isolated radar posts. My aim would have been to run as fast as I could over the mountains, or if I had to, ski over them – what a coward I was.

As I've already said the Americans were in charge of Iceland and so all of our food was American canned, which was brought to us from Reykjavik, and it was remarkably good stuff after rationing at home. It was the first time that I had tried canned bacon and I found it to be pretty good. Of course there was no set time for meals; we each cooked what we fancied on an open fire range, it was just like setting up some sort of routine from day to day. The first real task was to put the radar set in a little hut, built on a small ridge close to the campsite, and of course the main set was going to be housed at the top of the mountain. It was some three or four weeks before operation began and so a watch rotation had to begin. From then a few more sailors arrived, such as a telegraphist, a medic nurse and two cooks, so the size of the team, which was fifteen strong to begin with, was increased, not considerably but by a few more people. We already had a motor mechanic who had to look after the generators in the camp below and we used the top camp where another generator was housed. Toilet arrangements were very primitive – a large hole with a plank across found in one of the small huts. For washing we had just two taps, and hot water involved putting a bucket on the fire. Water was even more difficult in the top camp but I will talk a little about that when I come to actually living in the top camp, at the mountain top.

I must come back to the position of Saebol itself. When I tell you it was an isolated place I really mean isolation – there were just three farms there, a farmer and his wife living in these farms, and a small chapel. The children of the farmers were actually away working in other parts of Iceland and we rarely saw them. From the photographs you can see that there was absolutely nothing there, nothing whatsoever. It was a bleak spot, which I myself called a prison – a prison because although we weren't behind bars we had absolutely nothing to do and nowhere to go. But it was true that while we were there we were never paid; we drew a nice lump sum of money when we returned to Reykjavik to go home. We were able to purchase some cans of beer – there was a ration to the number you could have, I think it was either four or five cans a week – and cigarettes and chocolate. Now my memory will not allow me to recall how we paid for those things. I think it was that we were debited and that debit went to the naval establishment in Reykjavik to deduct from what we were going to get at the end of the assignment but I really can't remember. All I know is that we weren't paid any money and therefore we never had any money. Nothing to buy, nowhere to go, nothing to see, just pure and simply working together in what was called a secret station.

We had to start to get things to the top of the mountain. The first radar set was operational and we were in contact with Reykjavik, telling them what we were picking up, and they of course would tell us whether this or that was a friendly ship or one that we should continue to report to them. We first of all reported by telephone, but as said I earlier a telegraphist arrived, and then of course we were in touch with headquarters in Reykjavik by Morse code.

The railway track was for us to put stuff on; food had to go up there. There was already coal and diesel at the top but we had to take other items, the radar equipment and food etc., and we did that by helping to push the truck which was attached to a fairly large motor at the top. Then when it got to the top we had to transport it, I would think some half to three quarters of a mile, from the top to the actual site of the gun ring and the one fairly large ammunition hut and the other hut that had the generator in. And so supplies were slowly taken to the top and the radar mechanic was working on installing the set and getting it operational. Then we would be able to get a much longer range from the top of the mountain than what we could get from where the set was on the little ridge.

We used to have our post brought in around about once a month. We had supplies brought in on a regular basis, and we had a doctor who came in to inspect us and chat to us every two months. With regard to the mail, Peggy wrote to me every day. Not always a full letter, but she wrote something every day, all the time that I was away. Not only on this assignment but on other assignments, she wrote to me telling me what was going on – of course it was extremely difficult for me to reply, what could I tell her? Absolutely nothing. She didn't know where I was. She knew of course that I was somewhere rather cold, but as for anything else about where we were, what we were doing, what was happening, of course that could not be told. So I'm afraid that my letters were nowhere near as frequent as hers and certainly they were nowhere near as interesting. All she could gather from them was that I was still alive. She knew that the assignment was for twelve months and so she would know just how much longer I had to stay where I was. It turned out that I was there for thirteen months not twelve, which I had been told was the length of the draft.

Of course it was a part of the world that had extremes of light and of temperature. We went from almost twenty-four hours of light to almost twenty-four hours of darkness. When we first arrived we were coming up to the middle part of the year and so the weather was reasonable and we were able to, well I wouldn't say enjoy life, but we were able at least to move around. We could also do some fishing in the bay. Fishing brought us, quite easily, cod caught off a boat in that bay. It was an easy process, it didn't need any special technique or equipment, you just dropped the baited line over and in no time you would bring back a few nice sized cod. We got used to catching and then eating what was a delicious, fresh fish.

I called the place a prison; it was a prison in as much as, although there were no iron bars, there was absolutely nothing to do other than the jobs that kept the camp running and the business of going on watch in the radar hut which was on the ridge. We were busy at that time in getting stuff and supplies up the mountain and that took quite a bit of our time. Of course not everybody was going to finish at the same time because as I said there were fifteen of us to begin with, but slowly and surely the number of people staying there was enlarging the whole consignment of sailors. Lieutenant Lewis was the lieutenant in charge to begin with and some months later, I can't remember exactly how long, another lieutenant came along, Lieutenant Commander Carmichael. You'll notice from the photographs the number of people who were there in the beginning compared to the number of people who were there when I left at the end of thirteen months. Of course our object was to cover the convoys and ships that were going along from Reykjavik to Murmansk, as I've said before, and that was the main operation of the camp itself. We weren't having to do anything else, other than make certain that we stayed alive and that we were able to do a twenty-four hour watch, which was necessary in order to cover what the Admiralty wanted us to do. They were looking mainly for the German battle ships, which were apparently in that area.

Getting the supplies up the mountain was a fairly straightforward operation. It was the summer months and everything had to be up and running before the terrible winter which was to come. I can't quite remember exactly how long it took for the top camp to be operational. It would be a guess that it was some three months before everything was OK for us, for some people, to go and live at the top of the mountain in the mission hut which was provided for us. It was pretty close to the gun ring and the little hut with the radar set on top of it, on top of the gun ring. The gun ring itself was fairly close to the edge of the mountain which just dropped down into the sea, so you had to be careful that you didn't wander, other than going from the mission hut to the radar hut at whatever time of the night and day.

And so things went along quite like that for some time, very boring. The doctor came and I think it was after around about six months that he actually sent two people home because they were totally disturbed and were not able to continue with the operation. Of course supplies were brought in and our precious letters came from the UK. For my part, I could hardly tell Peggy anything, everything did have to be a secret. I never told her just how down I was – but I was.

In the early stages of course we had long hours of light. You could see the sun going down on the horizon, and then it was not very long before the sun rose again, making it into the next day. This was only going to be for a short time, although it didn't seem a short time to those of us who were there; every day seemed very long. However time did pass by and then we were getting into the autumn and then of course came the winter. By the time the autumn was over the snow started to fall and from then onwards, until I came home, I saw nothing but snow.

Mistakes were made. First of all, during the early part of the winter we couldn't get the engine at the top of the mountain started, and so everything that we were taking up there had to be transported by skis and sacks on our backs. We had to ski up the mountain and then across the plateau to the site itself. Even more difficulties came as the winter went on. The coal that was at the top of the mountain got frozen into the ground, we simply could not get it out, which meant that some coal had to be transported from the bottom camp to the top camp. Some of us, on our skis, had to take the coal up in sacks on our backs. Not easy at all, particularly in the depth of winter when temperatures went from minus a degree during the day to something like minus twenty-five at night. If you were travelling along this plateau towards the camp in a blizzard, well it was not the sort of thing you would want to experience too often. Unfortunately for us, we understood from the

Icelanders that the winter was a particularly bad one. The Icelanders could never understand how we were going to survive at the top of this mountain during the winter. As the time went on, as you can see from the photographs, the snow became thicker and thicker and temperatures dropped and dropped – we began to wonder ourselves just exactly how we were going to survive. In order to make certain that we were moving in the right direction round the place we had a torch and a compass. You simply had to walk in that direction, hoping that you were going to find the camp. Nobody ever did get lost or fall over the sides so I guess that particular operation worked perfectly, except of course that it was not very pleasant at all.

Saebol showing the mountain on which the radar operation was established

Living on top of the mountain

Some of first to arrive. I am the one with black socks

More snow

Digging out – a never-ending job

Water supply at the top of the mountain was simply us taking water up the mountains in jerry cans. In the mountain top camp water was very precious, so the washing of clothes and the business of keeping ourselves clean was not a priority in any shape or form. Water was for our cups of tea etc., and an occasional wash down from heating the water up on the fire. It was more plentiful in the winter because all our water supplies came from going outside, getting buckets of snow, bringing them back onto the fire and melting them.

On one occasion, I can't remember just when it was, I was suffering from a rather nasty tooth ache, and when the doctor came I told him. He said, 'Well, I'm not a dentist but I will have a go at getting it out, because that's the only way in which that pain is going to go away.' So he sat me down in a chair, opened my mouth, he obviously put an injection in my mouth and then for some time – which seemed like hours and hours – he was pulling and tugging trying to get this tooth out. How long it really took I don't know, but it was a long time and when it came out my face was black and blue. I was pleased to get the tooth out but I didn't feel too good after that operation.

We had an unfortunate incident when a convoy, which had obviously gone by, had been attacked. An American sailor was washed up, dead, onto our shore just into the harbour. We went down, found him and took his papers from him, and the Officer Lieutenant Lewis took them to report to the Admiralty. We made him a coffin, we did have wood supplies there, it was surprising what sort of supplies we did have, and we buried him in the little chapel. We had a short service and his name was forwarded to the Admiralty in order for them to carry out formalities. It was a sad occasion but then that is what happens during a war.

I saw the northern lights, the aurora borealis, on many occasions. It was a magnificent sight and the sort of thing you never forget, I can't recall just exactly how many times I saw it but it was quite often and a fascinating sight to see. Whether it was worth being in Saebol just in order to see the northern lights I'm not so sure.

The time was coming when my twelve months would be up and I would be returning home. Unfortunately, and I don't know why, those fourteen of us who went there in the first place did an extra month and so we didn't actually start to return to England from Saebol until we had completed thirteen months. Never the less it was exciting to be saying goodbye. We caught the boat to Reykjavik, where we only had some two or three days I think, before the troop ship bought us home, but in that time we were paid for our full thirteen months that we were entitled to. I really can't tell you the amount of money that was involved but it seemed to me that I was rich beyond compare. I'd got all this money and I was going home to see the person who meant so much to me. We got on the troop ship, this time the weather was very much kinder than coming out although there was still the chaos, too many people aboard the ship, and the difficulty of eating and sleeping, and the daily routine was something which you wouldn't imagine could happen when you're in the forces but it did. Some of my pals who were coming back with me got into a card school, and started to play for money which they could ill afford to lose. Sadly some of them lost more money than they should have done. I certainly didn't – my money was in my pocket and that was where it was going to stay until I got home.

I can't remember the dock that we went to, I'm pretty sure it was

Greenock, and then down to London then on to Portsmouth. We were only there for a day or two and I was then home on two weeks' leave. I went to my mother's first of all. Another surprise for me was that she had kept half of the allowance which the Admiralty had paid her every week for me, and she gave it to me on the day that I returned. I thought that was very nice of her, a person with her small means, that she only took half of what she was actually allowed.

The next day there was no way in which I could get in touch with Peggy at all, I had to wait until the next morning. I went to where she was working at St Pancras town hall, and what a reception I got when I went into the town hall and into her office. I was trembling with excitement and people there were hugging and kissing. I was now meeting up with the most special person I'd ever met, and somebody who meant the whole world to me. We were now going to be together for two whole weeks. It was decided that I would stay at Peggy's from the Monday to the Friday, because her father was on night work as I've told you before, and the bed which he occupied during the day was vacant. So Peggy slept with her mother and I slept in another room. There was no such thing then as sleeping together before one was married, that was absolutely off limits. Of course Peggy's father wanted to sleep with her mother over the weekends, and so I spent time with my mother on the Saturday and went back to Highridge Road on the Sunday. I could only tell you that both Peggy and I were now in another world. We realised that I had made it and we were now together, the one thing in the world that we both wanted, that I should come back and be safe and sound.

Of course Peggy was working. She was only able to get one week as a holiday and the first week was spent with her back at work but I would go up with her in the morning on the train and then I would stay in London. We would have lunch together and have a little walk in the park and then in the afternoon when she finished we came back together to Highridge Road. Having two weeks' leave at the beginning rather felt as though I had a whole lifetime with her and that the two weeks would never end. Of course that was foolish, but that was how one got over the time factors of being away and being together. We did nothing exciting because the war was still on, rationing was still about and there were still air raids, not so many in London but in other cities of the UK. So we were still in a war situation, and in any case, what mattered to us was that we were together, we were able to talk, we were able to be in each other's arms, we were able to talk about what had gone on over the past year. I obviously had to be careful what I told her but I think I told her enough that she realised the type of life I had been leading. They were among the most magical, magical weeks of my life.

It came to the second week, the week that she had as a holiday, and we started to talk about marriage, for the first time really. I was just about nineteen and she was twenty-one, and our thoughts turned to married life and how we would react when the time came for me to leave. We were on the top deck of a bus in Oxford Street, towards the very end of my leave, and I proposed marriage. How? I really cannot remember, it would not have been in a very romantic way but luckily she said yes, and from that moment we were engaged. I had no ring, so what we had to do was get off the bus, go into a jeweller's shop and decide what ring it would be in order to cement the engagement. At the time new rings were subject to what was called purchase tax, and so a second-hand ring was much cheaper and better value than paying the same amount for a new ring. Both Peggy and I have always been money conscious, and so we decided on a £20 second-hand ring. We didn't have the £20 on us, it was not the sort of money that we carried about, but of course I did have the money in my Post Office savings account. And so we went back to her office and spoke to Doris who was the personal assistant to the town clerk. Doris and Peggy were very good friends and she lent us the money knowing that it would be repaid in a day or two. We went back to the jeweller's shop, we bought the ring, I put it on her finger, and we were engaged.

That evening we had to go back to Highridge Road and tell Peggy's mother and father. What would happen was that we would be married the next time I came home, whenever that was going to be. It would be at least a year and possibly longer – and of course it was longer as it turned out. Peggy's mother and father were quite OK. I think they had begun to realise that their daughter and I were madly in love with each other, and that marriage was the only outcome.

Now we were coming to the end of my leave and a goodbye had to be faced. It was heartrending; neither of us knew if we would see each other again, neither of us knew how long I was to be away. We were just waiting for the war to end and for us to live together for the rest of our lives. The actual embrace and the departure when I left the house that particular morning were extremely sad. We hardly knew what to say, it was a question of being as brave as we possibly could. We looked at each other, we kissed, I said goodbye, she said goodbye. I turned around, I remember, and was going to go but when I got to the corner of the road I simply had to go back for just one more embrace, one more goodbye. I turned round again. I waved and I was away. Tears were not enough. Only the war itself would decide our future.

This was not a film where a director would be saying, 'Cut, let's go for a cup of tea.' This was real life – the touch, the feel, the holding of hands –

and scores of people were doing exactly the same as us. Saying goodbye and not knowing if that really meant goodbye for ever, perhaps never to see each other again. War is such a destructive event, and only those who have had the experience of war will know the emotions that one goes through day after day. That is why on Remembrance Sunday Peggy and I always think of those who did not return, because we both know from our own lives just what those people missed.

I was now in Portsmouth barracks, after the fourteen days' leave, and waiting for the next draft, which came along quite quickly. In fact it was less than a week before I was given the draft and told that it was to last two years. I would be sent to HMS *Guardian*, a net-laying cruiser which at that time was in dock in Belfast. So I needed to go from Portsmouth by train to Stranraer in Scotland, catch the ferry across from Stranraer to Larne, and then the train to Belfast. Of course this was going to be my very first ship. I had no great knowledge of routines aboard ship and would have to be what one would call a new boy at that time. I had to report to the master at arms, who on board a ship is the man who is responsible for organising discipline, etc. He is the senior lower deck man, just above a petty officer – not one of the officer command, but a very important man. He had to put each new sailor that came aboard into watch form, so that people knew when they could go ashore, when they were entitled to go on leave and the whole organisation of what went on when the ship was in harbour. There is a great deal of difference between the routine on board a ship while you're in harbour and the routine when you're at sea. I'll tell you a bit more about the routine at sea when we actually lift the anchor and sail away.

I was given the mess number that I was to join, and I went below decks with my kit bag and hammock and stowed them away in the appropriate places. My mess was a radar mess, where there were eight other people, seven of them just ordinary able seamen like myself and one leading seaman who was in charge of us on that particular mess, and also would be in charge while we were at sea. We very quickly got to know each other. I can only remember one or two names, I've never been good with names, but on the next mess deck to me was an ordinary seaman – well an able seaman really – and his name was Alf Gillis. Alf was a particular friend of mine the whole time that I was on the *Guardian*.

In the morning, while we were in Larne harbour, it was always piped for all the sailors to get onto the foredeck, and it was also piped as to what dress you would be wearing for that particular day. Every type of clothing in the navy had a number – if you were to wear overalls it would be piped. Number one was the best suit, your number one suit. So it would be piped at the beginning of the day by the boatswain what the uniform of the day was, then you would go to the foredeck and queue up with the boatswain in front. I knew we were going to go somewhere quite hot, because when I was given the draft I was also fitted out with clothing suitable for very much warmer weather than I had experienced in Iceland. So I was going from the very cold to the very warm – where, I did not know at that particular time.

There was the morning routine of the boatswain calling out 'fall out mess deck cleaners', 'fall out flat cleaners', 'fall out captain of the heads', on and on. Captains of the heads were two or three people who were in fact the toilet cleaners – of course aboard a ship it's not called a toilet, it's called a head. There were no doorways on the heads, or on the actual lavatories themselves, you sat there and did your business with anybody who was in there watching you. It was so everybody knew that there was nothing untoward going on in there. I quickly found that people disappeared in the mornings and there would only be just a few people left to do what was going to be the job of the day. It could be painting or scrubbing, or any sort of job which was necessary, mainly to keep people occupied. So I quickly became a captain of the head and when there was a call 'fall out captain of the heads' then I ran. I just went and got a broom and some cloth and that. Nobody took any notice of what you were doing or what was happening. As long as you were out of the way and you weren't causing any disturbance everybody was apparently happy, and that was life aboard while we were in harbour, totally different from when we were out at sea.

Of course every ship has a postman, a sailor who had been a sailor for some time, but of course just an able seaman on the lower deck, appointed by the master of arms at the time that he was organising the ship's company. While we were in harbour, the postman would go every day to collect the mail. I've told you before that Peggy wrote to me every day, at least a part of a letter every day, and so I did have plenty of mail and became known as the letter man. I kept her letters, they were something which was very close to me and something which I read and reread and reread again.

We waited in the morning for the instructions to be piped to see which watch was going to be allowed shore leave that night. Shore leave would be granted to port watch or starboard watch – well, port watch was port one or two and starboard one or two, so you knew when you were able to go ashore. Not only that, it would be piped what number clothing you would have to wear to go ashore. Of course in Belfast it was always, I think I'm right to say, number one, but while we were in other parts of the world, in warmer climates when we were in shorts and socks or had to wear a white suit, a different number would be called for those who were going ashore.

Round about five o'clock time, when we queued up to go ashore, everyone had their pay book with their identity, etc. on it and that had to be on a piece of string around your neck – it wasn't to be put in any pockets, it had to be safely round your neck and on your chest and that was inspected by the officer of the day. Of course they didn't want them to be lost, and found by people who could use them for other means.

It was not long before we were on our way. Two days before leaving harbour no one would be allowed ashore, obviously in order that we were all nicely sober to take to sea. Now at sea, we were divided again into different watches. There were eight of us, on four hours on and four hours off, and two would be portside, two would be on the starboard side on the bridge, where the radar sets were located. Four hours on and four hours off meant that in your four hours off you had to do everything; eat, get any washing done. While you were in your four hours off you were not allowed to take off any clothing, the only things you were allowed to take off were your boots.

We didn't sleep in hammocks, we just slept wherever there was a space on our mess or round our mess, either on the mess deck table or on the gangways or wherever there was room. The problem was that action stations were always at dawn or dusk. Even if there was no action to take place, action stations were piped for both of those, and of course at action station everyone had to be by their watch. So it could well mean that in your four hours off, if it happened to be in either the dawn or the dusk, you had to stand to, which would normally take about an hour or so before it was piped that it was all clear. Of course if there was real action then you weren't piped down until such time as the action was over.

After we had been out for some twenty-four hours it was piped that our next destination was Gibraltar and therefore from that moment onwards we all knew what that meant. Gibraltar, as you know, is the little rock at the bottom of Spain and is at the opening of the Mediterranean. It meant that we were going to be attached to those convoys transporting all sorts of foods and ammunition and so on to the people in Malta. As anybody who has read anything about the war at all knows, a siege took place in Malta and the people were starving. They had nothing at all. They did have aircraft there to try and fend off all the raids that were taking place but Malta itself was a country that was held by mostly Italians and of course Germans. I don't mean that they invaded the country, I mean that the shipping stopped supplies getting to them and slowly but surely they were reaching the brink of desperation.

We arrived in Gibraltar, I can't remember how many days we were at sea. I know from time to time it was pretty rough but then I always got seasick. I was always sick at sea in those first two or three days and slowly but surely got over it after that, although I have to tell you that in some very rough seas then everybody aboard was sick. When I'm talking about rough seas I mean really rough seas, not just a little wave here and there. We landed in Gibraltar and were tied up against the wall – sometimes in harbour you would be at anchor or sometimes tied up to a buoy, and in Gibraltar we were actually tied up against a wall. Gibraltar, if you've never been there, is just a lump of rock really and there's only one street, that's all there is. Of course to us it didn't matter too much, when we came ashore the first thing we were looking for was a bar or a club to have a drink. I would think, 'Oh well, thank goodness we've survived just what we've been through and have to hope that's what's going to happen on another day.'

What we the ship's company didn't realise of course, is that we were carrying a lot of ammunition, much more than we would normally carry. It was for two reasons – one was to get it to Malta and another was to have spare ammunition for the Americans who had some aircraft carriers, passenger ships which had been turned into aircraft carriers, and they couldn't carry enough ammunition. This was not known to the crew at that time, but it obviously had got out to somebody or another. While we were tied up alongside the wall there was an explosion aboard, down in the hold where a lot of this ammunition was, and we caught fire.

Now the captain was Captain Lane, a very much older man who had been brought back in to the naval service when the war began. He was, to be honest with you, a little bit past actually being in command of a ship, but that's another story. Of course emergency stations were called and I was on the bridge because that's where the radar sets were operated. I was quite close to the captain and he issued the instruction to abandon ship. I can tell you, and this is absolutely true, the first man who went down the gangway was the captain, the second man was his flunky with two cases and the third man was me. We got ashore and queued up, and some brave sailors stayed aboard and eventually put the fire out. I can't remember how long it took, but it was some time that we stood there and waited for the next instructions. The fire was put out and we then went back aboard and the captain piped that a mistake had been made – that he had never really instructed us to abandon ship, he was only thinking of it, and could we all understand that the instruction to abandon ship was in fact a mistake. What a laugh! What a scare it gave us too, that from that moment onwards we really knew the type of person who was in command of the ship. Everyone in the navy has a nickname, and anybody who was called Lane was called 'Shady', so he was always 'Shady Lane' as opposed to Captain Lane – not to his face of course.

For my own nickname I was always called Red, the reason being that at that time there was a very famous comedian, an American, called Red Skelton, everybody knew of him. So I was never called John. That's what happens in the navy, somebody who is Mr White would be Chalky and so on.

By this time, while we were in harbour, we had set up a radio station for the ship's company. I wasn't part of the actual set-up itself but I was a regular contributor because I was able to sing quite well really, all the old favourites like 'We'll meet again', 'Apple blossom time', and 'You are my sunshine'. There was one particular favourite of the ship's company, a comical song about the elephant's bottom – with which I won a competition in the Fleet Club in Alexandria.

The time came when we were going to leave harbour. Nobody had any idea exactly where we were going, although Malta was pretty obviously our next destination. We joined into a convoy with quite a number of ships which came from other ports as well as from Gibraltar, I can't tell you how many ships there were but there were quite a number. I'll say this about the journey, it wasn't pleasant. Once or twice we were on sort of stand-by for some twenty-four hours or even longer, but eventually those who survived actually got to Malta. We arrived there long after the famous oil tanker, the SS *Ohio*. She was destined for Malta some months previously, and had gone through some horrific bombardments on the way. She did eventually get to Malta, quite badly damaged, and they did unload the oil, but *Ohio* then sank in Valletta harbour. We were there some time after that particular incident.

The people in Malta were very hard done by, I suppose destitute is a phrase that you could use. Two days before we arrived in Malta itself, the instruction was piped that we were not to throw any food away – that anything which left by us was to be kept in buckets. When we got into Valletta harbour they allowed the children to come aboard, children only of course, and they took away all this scrap food, can you imagine? Being one or two days old, and all it was was the leftovers from people's plates, they were taking that back, these children were taking that back to their homes. I will always remember that.

I have a story which I'll tell you now, although it happened many years later while I was on holiday in Malta, because Peggy and I went there two or three times. Sitting next to me on a seat in Valletta itself was a man of a similar age to me, or perhaps somewhat younger. We started talking and he remembered coming aboard those ships as a child, and collecting that food. He didn't remember which ship he went aboard, he didn't know whether he had come aboard HMS *Guardian* or not, but he remembered those ships.

And he hugged me and said, 'You've absolutely no idea, no idea what that food meant to us, we were still a country under siege and every little speck of food was in fact so gratefully received.' There were tears in his eyes; he couldn't say thank you enough for the way in which we allowed them to come aboard and take, well almost rubbish, back for them to eat.

Our next port of call was to be in Port Said, Alexandria and from there we went to Beirut in the Lebanon. We had an organised trip over the mountains into Syria. Damascus was the place that we went to and there is a photograph of us throwing snow balls at each other. Remember that it was summertime, but we were throwing snow balls at the top of this mountain at each other as we were on our way to Damascus. It was a day trip, that was all, and then we came back to Beirut. The only reason I'm mentioning Beirut is because, of the scores of places I have been to, Beirut at the time was the nicest of them all, head and shoulders above anywhere else that I'd seen previously and certainly anywhere else that I'd seen after I'd been there – a very elegant, posh seaside resort. I shall always remember it in that way.

Snowballing on an outing from Beirut to Damascus in Syria

We came out of Beirut and then went back to Malta. Now I've got to deal with two specific items – the Italian fleet surrender and of course the Greek mutiny which took place while I was there. My recollections of it are not great, but I do know that we were involved in both of those incidents. The Italian fleet actually surrendered in September, on the 10th of September 1943, and of course I was in the Med at that time. The Italian fleet, which I have researched, did surrender in Malta at that time. I have a photograph that I'm sure is of an Italian admiral coming aboard us to do something or other, whether it was to sign anything I don't really know. I do know that in the records HMS *Guardian* is not actually recognised, but never the less we were in that particular area when the Italian fleet surrendered. Now the Greek mutiny, again I've researched and that took place in two parts. Part of it was in Malta and the other part was in Port Said, just beside Alexandria. The photographs I have got are marked Port Said, and they are photographs of us sailors who were kitted out with army gear and a rifle and a bayonet. You can see from the photographs that we were ready for anything that might take place, and we did go aboard one ship – not that it was a very mutinous type of situation, but it was just to show them that we were there and we were protecting the officers with regard to the actual mutiny.

Alf Gillis ready for action

What I do know for certain is that from there we went to Malta and we were in Malta, in St. Pauls Bay, for some two months. Here you'll see the photographs of the ships that we were guarding, and they were either the Italian fleet or the Greek fleet, I cannot remember which. We didn't go to sea, we stayed in St. Pauls Bay, quite a small town of course with very little to do. We swam off the ship, we played water polo, we played football, we went sailing and we even played cricket. The *Guardian* had a very large afterdeck and we even managed to play cricket on the afterdeck. In the photograph of me at the time you can see that I was physically fit, and if anybody had asked

Boarding party ready for action

me I felt as though I could have pushed over a house. I wouldn't say it was a pleasant time because there was really nothing to do, nothing happened, nowhere to go really and so the two months did drag on. In the end we left St. Pauls Bay and went back to Alexandria.

A Greek ship

53

Greek officers leaving HMS *Guardian*

Nineteen and feeling fit in Malta

Everyone who was in the Malta convoys was allowed to have what they called a rest holiday. This particular camp was in Massawa in Eritrea and that meant we had to go through the Suez Canal from Port Said to Port Tawfik and then down the Red Sea to Eritrea and Massawa. The idea was that half the ship's company would go to the camp for four days and then the other half would have their own four days. We went up by lorry into the mountains, and the temperature was much more sociable than what it was down in the Red Sea, so we could enjoy the fact that we weren't perspiring for most of the day. The idea of the holiday was that there was absolutely no discipline, the bar was open for twenty-four hours of the day, we had our own bed to sleep in, we had somebody come in who would do our washing for us, and we were just able to do anything we liked. If you wanted to sleep all day you could, or there was a snooker table, table tennis, all sorts of activities. I can assure you that there were many drunken sailors during the days that we were in this holiday camp.

Just round the corner from our camp was a tribal village, quite a dirty village really, not the sort of place that you would want to go to and live, that was absolutely certain, but of course we went there. Where there was a young lady available, outside the tent they would put a red flag. I can assure you that the greater majority, in fact I would think it was almost ninety-nine per cent, would never have entered those huts, but there was one particular guy, Chalky White, a man of about thirty I would think. He had no attachments, he treated life just as though it was a whole adventure and once or twice he certainly went into the tent where the red flag was flying outside. The question of a venereal disease never entered his mind. That was the one thing that turned sailors away from that sort of thing, the question of catching a disease. There was no such thing then as penicillin or anything like that which would cure things in a matter of days, and there were plenty of people aboard who went through some pretty horrific treatment. That was a decisive enough factor for the majority of us to stay away from that sort of behaviour. As far as I was concerned of course, I knew that when I got home I was going to be married and so the decision was quite easy for me.

On our way back we called in at Alexandria again and we stayed there for some time, doing what, really I couldn't tell you, but we were in harbour. In Alexandria there were a lot of troops from the North African Eighth Army etc., and airmen, and there was a club called the Fleet Club. On any one night there would be some two thousand, possibly more, people in the Fleet Club. The idea was that when you went to the bar you ordered the number of bottled of beer that you were going to drink through the whole evening, You certainly didn't want to queue up more than once and so you had the caps taken off the bottles of beer, but then of course you needed bits of paper etc. to block the top just to stop the beer from going flat. And so, on every table, you would find scores upon scores of bottles of beer. I can't remember the numbers we used to consume, I wasn't a great drinker. I had my share but I wasn't one that was over the top too often. However, at this club there was always what was termed a 'sod's opera', where people would get up onto the stage to sing and tell jokes etc. The winner was decided by the amount of clapping from those who were competing. As I've told you before, I could sing a bit and I had done two or three songs previously at the Fleet Club, but on one occasion I sang the comical song called The elephant's bottom and I won. There was a prize, I can't remember what it was, but I was quite pleased that at last I had won the competition with the elephant song.

During my time in the Med we went to quite a lot of other places like Taranto and Brindisi in Italy, and Algiers, and of course quite often Alexandria and Malta. Then came the shock to me. I was called into the captain's cabin and he told me that I was about to leave the ship. I was leaving the ship because, unbeknown to me, I had been tested as to whether I would be a suitable candidate to become an officer. I would be catching a troop ship back to England.

Now this was a two-year commission, so I was going back after eighteen or nineteen months. I now realised why once or twice I had to take a class of sailors and drill them up and down, turn left and turn right etc. etc. I'd had interviews with the navigation officer and interviews with the gunnery officer, and that sort of thing. I thought that was just all part and parcel of becoming a seaman, but apparently it was more than that. I was being judged as to whether I was a suitable candidate to become a naval officer and on the card that I came back to England with it stated that I was being relieved of my duties on HMS *Guardian* to sit the Admiralty selection board. A big surprise to me, a big surprise to other people who were aboard – it was a

Myself and Alf Gillis

57

moment when my thoughts were only that I was on my way back home to Peggy.

My pal Alf Gillis took it a little badly because we had become very close friends, and he was surprised that this happened, he'd had no idea and neither did I. Before I left he gave me a book. It was the full works of Shakespeare, quite a large book and I could see that he had bought it in the Fleet Club in Alexandria because it was marked inside there with that name. In it he wrote, 'With all the best wishes and success and happiness in your future life, to one of my very few real friends, your oppo Alf Gillis.' As he gave it to me he also said, 'I hope when I see you next time that I've got to salute you.' I thought that was rather touching.

6

I left the ship and went into the camp where I was going to stay for the next couple of weeks or so in Alexandria, waiting for the troop ship home. I can tell you it was a hell hole, it wasn't really a camp at all in the true sense of the word because we were in the desert, and we were living under canvas. The whole place was bug infested to such an extent that every morning we had to burn the bugs that used to crawl up and down the bed from the sand.

There was no flooring, just the sand and a bed. There were some facilities for washing and things like that and you kept your kit bag in the tent. From time to time we'd take our kit bags for a debugging process. I don't quite know what they did but all of our gear was debugged and we were debugged as well. I know that I never took all my clothes off at night, I was always covered from head to foot in order to try and keep the little swines from crawling all over me.

It was not the most pleasant time of my life. There was nothing to do of course, I was simply waiting with lots of other people who were also waiting for this troop ship. I have forgotten what I did for any sort of recreation, other than every day seemed like a week. I must have been there for some two weeks or so before I caught the troop ship back to the UK. What kept me going at that time was that I knew that I was going back, that I was going to marry, and at least as long as I was safe on the troop ship I thought, well I've made it once again. So eventually I was on my way back to England, and the normal chaos took place on the troop ship. It was the same aboard each one that I was on, you just muddled through to arrive at the other end.

Looking back over the whole episode of my Mediterranean trip I can recall one very sad moment and one when I was really taken by surprise. The sad moment was the day that I received the letter from my mother, I think it was about the middle of 1943, to say that my grandfather had died. You will recall the very fond affection that I had had from him from the beginning of my story. I must say that day was a very sad one for me and it will always be in my memory bank.

The letter that gave me the big surprise was when I received the photographs from the officer in charge in Saebol at the secret experimental station. He took the photographs of course, we weren't allowed to take them. He sent photographs of the camp and the people in the camp and the type of weather, etc. that we had to endure. He sent those to the first fifteen men who went with him to start the camp up. It was Lieutenant Lewis who was the man in charge, he took the photographs and I thought that it was a wonderful gesture for him to send them to those men who went with him on that first assignment.

I can't tell you how long it took me to get from Alexandria back into barracks; I've really no recollection of the length of time, all I know is that it seemed like a lifetime. Peggy didn't know that I was on my way back but she did know through my letters that I had been selected to become a naval officer, and of course she was pleased about that but she now had to wait for me to return home. When I got into the barracks I had to have an interview with the lieutenant commander who was going to be responsible for me and the sitting of the Admiralty selection board. He asked me what my intentions were on my leave, and he was aghast when I told him that I was going to get married. He said, did I realise that I was only twenty years of age, that if I went into an officers' mess there would be substantial fees, and that if I was there and I was a married person it would not be the right thing. He left me feeling without any shadow of a doubt that the choice was either to become a naval officer or to get married. I knew what the decision would be but it played on my mind. I found the whole thing rather difficult to deal with – never the less that's what I had to do.

So I arrived back home to 57 Highridge Road at around nine o'clock at night. I knocked on the door and the person who answered it was Peggy's Aunt Ciss who was living there, evacuated there with her little boy from London. She nearly collapsed, then she called to Peggy, who came to the door without any make-up on. She also had a couple of iron things that she used to put in her hair to make it wavy. It didn't matter to either of us how we were. I'd survived, she had waited for me and we were without any shadow of a doubt going to get married.

I think it was on a Tuesday that I arrived back and of course from then onwards it was all systems go, because the marriage would now take place on the Saturday. In those days you could get married with a quick licence for people who were serving soldiers, sailors or airmen. The people in the Methodist chapel that Peggy and her mother of course knew very well were absolutely wonderful because they played a major part in providing the food for the wedding breakfast and the flowers, etc. It was a team effort, most of which came from Peggy's family but also the chapel goers as well.

I found the first day or so a little difficult and Peggy realised this. I'd got to make up some story – I'd got to make up a story which sounded reasonable. I certainly wasn't going to say to her that I was either to be a naval officer or I was to be a married man. That was entirely out of the question. I'd made up my mind that I was to be married and married I would be. And so I thought of the story that I was caught coming out of the barracks with more cigarettes in my bag than I should have had, and therefore I was put under a suspect case. I could go on leave but I would have to suffer the consequences when I went back. I told Peggy and my family and friends that there was no question of going before the Admiralty selection board – for now, that was not going to happen.

I didn't worry about it; I didn't worry about it at all really. You have to remember that, by November 1944, it looked as though the war was being won and that it would be over sometime during 1945 and I had no intention of being a naval man when the war was over. It was my intention to leave just as soon as I possibly could and so it was not a big decision for me. I knew exactly what I should do.

Of course, Peggy had to go to work on the Wednesday and Thursday, to complete any work that was on hand, but mostly to see her friend Doris who was a very good friend indeed. She apparently organised a subscription list for our wedding, and although the sum of money seems small now I can assure you that in today's money it would be considerable. Doris was also apparently the organiser of the hotel in London where we were going to stay overnight on the Saturday, our wedding night. She also paid for two tickets for an evening visit to the cinema. The honeymoon was to be in Cleveleys which is a mile or two from Blackpool, in the house that Peggy's Uncle Percy lived in during the war with his wife and daughter Audrey. They were going to stay in Hemel after the wedding and leave the house to Peggy and myself.

I have to tell you that during those few days before the wedding I was totally bewildered, in fact useless. I did not know where the confident young man named John Skelton had gone but he had left behind this useless wreck. I did not know how the arrangements were going, how my family was told, how the best man was told, and so on and so on. I knew that Peggy's mother had made the dress. I knew what time I had to be at the church – in fact the night before I stayed in one of their chapel friends' houses, a Mr and Mrs Andrews who lived just down the road, and they were instructed to have me at the chapel on time. My sister Doreen was to be a bridesmaid; in fact she had been an evacuee with Peggy for a year while I was away, so they knew each other very well. The other bridesmaid was Peggy's best friend Doreen Surridge and on the wedding day they were both looking absolutely wonderful.

The day came, and I have to tell you this. I do not remember a single thing about the ceremony or the wedding breakfast, except for one thing. I remember looking round when Peggy was walking up the aisle, and I saw this wonderful dress and this beautiful young lady walking towards me. I do remember getting into the taxi to go to the station, I do not remember getting on the train, I do not remember the name of the hotel or the booked cinema or what film we saw. The day really just passed me by. However, I do remember feeling that it was the most wonderful day of my life, the day that I was going to be married to this very special person.

When the wedding was over Peggy's father came to me, shook my hand and said, 'You will look after her won't you?' I replied, 'Of course I will,' and that is what I tried to do for the rest of our lives together. In fact we were both of the same mind, we would look after each other. From the very beginning we realised that we were meant for each other, we were completely in tune with each other's feelings. When I was needed I was there, when Mummie was needed she never failed. We were a complete partnership.

The great day

Now comes the undressing, getting into bed ... It was not a great success, being the two virgins that we were it was not the best way to start. It was a disaster. However, happily I have to tell you that, on the honeymoon, Peggy was a tiger and things could not have been better between us. That carried on during the whole of our lives together, in fact even up to the last few weeks of our marriage when she was in her eighties Peggy would say on a regular basis, 'Take me to bed and give me a cuddle.' I think I will say no more on this subject.

During the day we went down to the long road on the promenade and caught the train to Blackpool, walked along north pier to the end which was covered with a glass roof, and listened to the band in comfortable deck chairs. The weather could not have been better. We also danced in the town ballroom and went to the cinema and theatre, but Peggy's favourite place was to be on our own in Uncle Percy's house. In later years, much later in fact, we tried to revisit the house but we could not remember the number, although we were certain of the road. Many times when our daughter Lesley had moved to Blackpool we tried to find it by various means, including having our story put in the local newspaper, but without success so far.

Of course we had to leave eventually and I had to go back to barracks. There was not so much tension as previously – we were winning the war and Peggy and I had survived. Of course with Peggy working in London she was subjected to the V1 and V2 rockets on a regular basis, something I did not realise when I was away but which I found out when I got home.

Arriving in Portsmouth barracks I had no charge to answer but I did have to see the same officer who had spoken to me before I went on leave, when I told him my plans for marriage. He was very considerate and under-standing of my predicament, but there was no alternative then. However he said he would transfer me to Devonport and I would await a place on the next Radar Plotting Instructors course, which would mean that I would not have to go to sea again. He actually told me that according to the records I had been a credit to the navy. I did find out, when I was discharged and received my naval records, that in my annual assessment in each of the five years my conduct was marked very good and that in the column efficiency and rating, just two years were marked satisfactory, the next three were superior. So I was on my way to Devonport and I stayed there for some time. Peggy even came to Devonport for a weekend stay and so we had another mini honeymoon. Eventually at the end of March I went to Douglas in the Isle of Man which was named HMS *Valkyrie*, to start my course.

HMS *Valkyrie* was actually a hotel on the promenade, taken over by the navy for this particular radar course, very comfortable really except that every day we had to march, well walk really, to the top of Douglas Head where the school was. Here I met the Queen Mother, who spoke to me about the radar set. What surprised me was the amount of make-up on the King's face, just like a model. He must have looked ill really, as we all discovered afterwards that he was suffering from cancer. When I was on the

Isle of Man, VE day came at the beginning of June of course, and the tremendous celebrations appeared to be nonstop. Soon after we had a victory parade though the main street. If you watch the Remembrance performance at the Albert Hall, well you might notice that when the Navy marches across the stage there is often someone out of step. You should have seen us as we marched past the main stand. Before we marched past the main marine band we were doing well, but just before the main stand they changed the tune. What a mess, what a shambles, what a calamity. I will say no more.

I passed the first part of the course quite well really and I then had to be transferred to HMS *Dryad*, a shore establishment just the other side of Portsmouth. I went there in the early part of July. It was while I was there that I learnt that Peggy was pregnant and that our first child would be born at the end of December. While I was at HMS *Dryad* VJ day came and the war was over. It made every bit of difference to the way in which life was going to be from that moment onwards. I left HMS *Dryad* and went back to Devonport and then I was transferred to HMS *Gold Crest*, which was along the Pembrokeshire coast in Wales, in Haverfordwest. There I was going to become an instructor as I'd just passed the course, but it was really quite irrelevant because the war was over and the only thing on people's minds was when we were going to be demobilised. Whatever I did as an instructor, and I did take some classes, most of the time really you could say that I was wasting my time and of course wasting theirs. I did have two seven-day leaves while I was at HMS *Gold Crest* but really very little happened that was of any importance. Peggy by this time had left work, mostly on the basis that she suffered rather badly from morning sickness and was unable to continue working. There was no such thing in those days as maternity benefits or anything like that when you gave up work through pregnancy etc. That was the end of your time at the particular company that you worked for.

Then came the time towards the end of December when they found that the baby was in fact in the wrong position, he was not head first but legs first. On the night that he was born, which was 31 December 1945, a strange thing happened. I was in my bed and I felt considerable pains in my stomach, in fact it was so bad that I had to go down to the sick bay. They kept me in the sick bay that night, and that was the very night Martin was born. It was unfortunately a very difficult birth. He was the wrong way round and as it was going to take place at home there was only a midwife present, and she attempted to induce the baby in these difficult conditions. These days it would never have taken place at home, once they found that Martin was a breach baby Peggy would have been taken to hospital. She paid for that for the rest of her life really, because it ruined her back, the trauma of the birth. But when Martin arrived on the scene he was a real little wreck and hardly living.

I learnt this when I received the telegram the next day after the birth to say that he was born. That meant that I would have four days' leave and I went home to find Peggy in this rather sad state and Martin in an even sadder state. There were bruises on him and he looked a very frail creature indeed. He needed a lot of care and attention; I suppose these days you would say TLC. Fortunately of course Peggy wasn't on her own, she was there with her mother and father, and so I rather felt that she would be in good hands. It was an extremely worrying time for us although at the same time we were pleased that our son was born and that he was named Martin John, Martin being after one of Charles Dickens' characters. Peggy was a great reader of Charles Dickens.

There is little more to be said really on what was happening in Haverfordwest, except that the only subject we talked about was when we were going to be demobilised. There was a rota system according to age, how long you'd served and all that sort of thing, but we didn't really know until some ten days or so before we were going to be demarked, and what date it would be exactly for any particular person to be released. In the few days before you actually left, you had to go to the demobilisation centre and choose a suit, a shirt, a coat, a trilby and a pair of shoes etc. So you were all ready to go home as a civilian, the end of the war had come. Mine was in the March of 1946. I was sent home. Of course war restrictions were over – the sort of secret things that you couldn't talk about. I could write and say what day I was going to be demobilised, when I'd be arriving home and so it wasn't unexpected like a leave used to be, when no one knew when their husband was coming home. Of course when I got back home everybody I saw was very pleased and there was great rejoicing, as there was in all families where the person who had fought in the war had survived and was now home as a civilian.

7

However it's not as easy as you might imagine being demobilised. You have got to settle down to a difficult type of life. For four, five, six years you have lived under very difficult and different circumstances. Now you've got to settle in to family life.

It was not generally an easy thing, and my situation was somewhat worse, because Peggy was in fact still troubled, and was troubled for the rest of her life, with her back, and of course Martin was a sick child and needed a lot of attention. So Peggy had once again come under the influence of her mother, and of course her mother had been with Martin since his birth and she had almost taken control really. I could understand that, because Martin was really the surrogate for the boy that Peggy's parents had had before, who had died when he was about fourteen months old. Martin had obviously taken the place of Donald and so Peggy's mother in some way became the mother of Martin.

When I came back it was difficult to reconcile the whole situation in which I found myself. We were in a small bungalow and there were difficulties, that is for certain. Such difficulties that after some few weeks Peggy and I had a long discussion about it. She knew how I felt, and we did discuss the question of whether I should go home to my mother for perhaps a couple of days a week and then come back. It never got to that, it was only talked about. We did have to live in the bungalow and we were all in close proximity to each other. Anyone who knows anything about a family living like that will know that it doesn't always come as an easy project. Now our concern was to find a place of our own.

It also meant of course that I was now going to have to find employment, but what was I going to do? Once again I was not in any way qualified to do anything that required working with my hands and I had to look for some office employment. In those days Hemel Hempstead was a very small town. There were less than twenty thousand people, the main shopping centre was in the High Street, and the town hall was at the top of the High Street. There was no industrial area or anything like that, and there were just two main employers, John Dickinson, the paper manufacturer, and Kent's Brushes. Almost everybody seemed to be somebody who worked at John Dickinson's, they were the large employers of the town.

There was no real argument between Peggy and I, we were just too pleased to be together. She understood my position and it was just a question that we had to overcome two problems: the first was to try and find accommodation, and the second was for me to get some employment. We didn't have any money worries because I had got my war gratuity and I was paid up by the navy until the sixth of June. We were just happy that we had both survived the war, we were together and we both realised that the sort of love that we had for each other would last a lifetime, and of course, everyone realises now that it did.

I was never what one would call despondent; I knew that my self-confidence had returned and that, given half a chance I would make a success of our lives. When people used to say to Peggy, 'Are you worried?' she used to say, 'No, John will know what to do. He will sort it out. I don't have to worry.' She must have said that throughout her life countless times and I hope that throughout that time I didn't let her down. I know that I always did the best for us as a family and that is how we survived during the whole of our lifetime together.

Now I was seriously looking for employment. I did write to John Dickinson's but I was not successful. However during that time we had a little bit of luck. In Hemel as elsewhere there was a shortage of shops where people could get their normal shopping done and so it meant that there was always a constant supply of people who came round the doors selling greengrocery, hardware or anything that you could buy in a shop. There was one person, a man named Sid Kerry, and he came around with quite a smallish van really, with hardware stuff and in particular he sold paraffin oil. Most people in those days used paraffin for lots of things, for lighting, for heating. Sid was a regular weekly caller to 57 Highridge Road. He knew of our circumstances, and one day he said that he knew of a lady at number 3 Cemmaes Court Road who had to find some new tenants in a matter of a few weeks for an apartment in her house. It only consisted of a living room and a bedroom, and of course a kitchen. He spoke to us about it and he also liaised with this particular lady and we went and saw the property. I wouldn't like to say that it was the cleanest house we'd ever been in but we weren't too worried about that – what we wanted was a place of our own and I think that, at that particular point in time, we'd have taken anything. So it was arranged that when this apartment became vacant Peggy and I and Martin would move in.

To go back to the business of people calling at the house, Peggy's father had a man who used to call on his bike. We called him the bookman, as he used to have a case full of books on the back of his bike. He used to call on Peggy's father every week and Peggy's father, from this case of books, would choose a book which would last him the week. It was the sort of thing that would not happen now.

I am afraid that I cannot recollect exactly when the next events took place. I would think it was most probably in July when I saw an advert in the local paper for a job in the stores of a company called the Electrical Apparatus Company, EAC Ltd, in St. Albans. Of course St. Albans was not just round the corner, it meant travelling. However, it appealed to me – it was a job to get me started, and so I wrote away and I had an interview with a man named Charles Kingston. He was the personnel manager at that time and he obviously liked me and took me on. I can remember my wages, they were £5 a week. I was to be a store man and my hours would be from seven-thirty in the morning until five o'clock at night. I can't say that I was over pleased by what I had obtained, but it was a job.

So there was a bit of a flurry. I was going to start work and we were going to move, although of course we were moving into furnished accommodation and so there was not a great deal that was going to be taken from Highridge Road to Cemmaes Court Road. The two things happened almost simultaneously. We settled into Cemmaes Court Road and I had to settle into employment in St. Albans. First of all I used to travel by bus from Hemel to St. Albans but of course that added expense to the family weekly budget. Once again I reverted to having my own bicycle and for the number of years that I worked at EAC I cycled backwards and forwards from Hemel to St. Albans every day. Weather did not deter me, I used to get up early, at least I used to leave the house by about six o'clock or so in the morning and then get back to Hemel around about half past six or so. While we were in Cemmaes Court Road we only had Martin of course, and when I got back I used to help with bathing Martin and putting him to bed because of Peggy's back.

We made the most of our time at Cemmaes Court Road, we were not downhearted. It wasn't the most palatial home that we could have thought of but we were together and we were happy. Unfortunately we were having to care for quite a sickly child. Martin was never a robust child, and I'll tell you more about that as the story unfolds.

I got on well at EAC, I fell into the routine in the stores and I made the most of the job that I'd got. Then towards the end of the year we found that Peggy was pregnant again. This was something quite unexpected and we were not too sure how to deal with it because after Martin's birth it was thought that she should think very carefully about having any other children. Well it had happened and so we were now confronted with dilemmas about what we were going to do.

There was never a question of termination, but there were questions being asked as to how we could reduce the chance of a miscarriage without too much danger. The medical opinion was that it had to be our decision whether to go ahead with this pregnancy and the risks involved and that's what we did. We simply had to make the most of something that we didn't particularly want to happen but there it is, it was going to happen and we allowed it to take its course. We were on the council housing list and we were regular visitors to the housing department at the town hall trying to put forward our case. The pregnancy did in fact help us towards getting accommodation from the council.

Now the timing of our move from Cemmaes Court Road into 49 Hobbs Hill Road is beyond my recollection. I have tried, through the council, to find the date that we actually moved in. It was a new house, a three bedroom house, and Hobbs Hill Road is along Belswains Lane and close to the Bennetts End area. I would say that it was possibly January or February when we moved in. There were a number of houses, I would think about ten or twelve, something like that, which were completed and people were all moving in at round about the same time. It did mean that we needed furniture and other odds and ends which of course everybody knows are needed when you move into a house for the first time. Peggy's mother and father were extremely helpful in this respect, but the majority of what we were going to buy would certainly have been on a hire purchase basis. There weren't things such as refrigerators, television sets, washing machines or anything like that in anybody's household, they were unheard of at that particular time. So what was necessary was simply something to sit on in the evenings and somewhere to sleep at night, and on wages of five pounds a week and with little other support, one had to be very careful with budgeting. Both Peggy and I were very good at that, we never found ourselves in the sort of debt which unfortunately many young couples do through easy credit etc. We didn't have that, we didn't have a lot of money but we were able to manage.

I was still working at EAC and getting along quite nicely. I was lucky that the people I worked with were the sort of people that I enjoyed being with. Eventually after many months I was offered a step up the ladder and it came at about the same time as our son Roland was born, which was on 28 May 1947. The birth this time was not as bad, but there were still difficulties and it was decided by the medical opinion under no circumstances should Peggy have another child. In order to make certain that this didn't happen she was fitted with some sort of coil arrangement. I was going to get some pro-motion, and I was extremely pleased. I was called into the personnel manager's office and he told me that now there was an opportunity to come and join the works management team, a big surprise to me. I would be a junior of course and I would join what was called the outside work controllers department, which dispatched to outdoor workers the parts for them to assemble, also to two or three companies and many just ordinary outworkers, and then for them to be placed in the appropriate departments when they came back. There were four of us, I was the youngest one and so I was given those sorts of duties which meant I was travelling about the factory chasing up parts and so on.

I cannot recall the amount that my wages increased. I know I was extremely happy about it when I related it to the amount of rent that I was paying, which, if my memory serves me right, was ten and sixpence per week, although it could have been twelve shillings and sixpence per week. I met quite a number of people when I travelled around the factory and I became known to a lot of people. I met a man there who was the under foreman of the maintenance department, his surname was Fellowes but he was always known as 'Trotter' Fellowes because he always walked around with his cap on, in a dirty pair of overalls with a spanner in his hand. No one ever saw him actually carrying out any maintenance work but he used to trot around the factory. Everybody knew Trotter Fellowes, he was a very nice guy and I got on with him very well. We had lots of laughs together. The important fact really is that my daughter Jackie eventually married his son, of course many years after I left EAC.

Going into a new house meant that there was a lot of work to be done, particularly on the garden. We had a front garden, we had a side garden because our house was at the end of four, and a very large back garden. From the back door was a covering which had a brick-built coal bunker as we were still using coal in those days and a brick-built shed with windows. It was quite a large sort of building where you could put your gardening tools etc. I was lucky because although I knew absolutely nothing about gardening Peggy came from a family of very good gardeners who knew quite a lot about horticulture and of course her father was a good gardener. Most people during the war with the severe rationing had to grow a lot of their own fruit and vegetables and he kept chickens as well, and so Peggy had a very good grounding in horticulture. She knew when plants should be going in and what seeds to buy and so I was very much guided by her as to the garden layout.

The first job was to make a concrete path from the back door to the bottom of the garden because that's where the washing was to be hung out and of course it was all virgin soil and was quite muddy when the rain came.

And so what I had to do first of all was to dig the trench and fill it with some broken bricks from the top of the garden to the bottom. Then came the business of how to actually get the concrete, which was quite easily overcome because they were starting to build some more houses in Hobbs Hill Road. So I, with a few other people as well, one particular Sunday, took a bucket to the building and filled it up with cement and sand etc., brought it back and mixed it up to make this concrete path. I knew that it was a fairly safe thing to do on a Sunday and so I did spend the whole of one Sunday making this pathway, going backward and forwards to collect the materials. In fact it's a path that stayed the test of time, because it lasted us while we were there, and some time ago I visited 49 Hobbs Hill Road and the pathway was still there.

I think the time has come that I should tell you the stories about my capabilities as a DIY specialist. These stories have circulated through the family over the years and always on the basis that Dad is not very good at DIY. The first was when I cut through an electric cable with a pair of pliers and I found myself on the other side of the room, I was thrown there from the electric shock. The next one was when I made some shelves with doors on the cupboard below in a recess. These shelves were going to house the complete set of encyclopaedias which we had bought for the boys at some time or another. The only problem was that when you opened the doors, the shelves and the books fell out onto the floor. I said, 'Well, what the hell do you want to open the doors for?' and my son Roland said, 'How do we get to the books without opening the door?' I said, 'Well, it looks very nice with the doors closed so let's just keep it closed.'

The third story is, I suppose, the one that is told the most. I was putting a pelmet up against one of our windows and I could not find a tape measure. So to measure it I put one hand against one side of the window and the other hand on the other side of the window. I tried to keep them in that position, got down from the ladder, and measured the piece of wood that I had to cut using that particular measure. I can tell you that I wasn't far out. It was only a little bit short. I am rather ashamed of how I overcame the problem that the pelmet was a little bit short, so I will not describe it, although it did last the whole of the time that we were in that house.

I'll not mention DIY again, you can tell from those stories that it was not my cup of tea and it was much better that I left those sorts of things alone. Peggy was always telling me about how good her father was at DIY, anything that wanted fixing he would fix, anything that wanted doing he would do it straight away. However, for me it was not one of my strong points, in fact even today I can lift the bonnet of a car up and look inside and not know anything at all about what I'm actually looking at. It's just a jumble of different wires and different objects put together. No, I leave the DIY to other people.

8

I was making good progress at EAC and I got on very well with the management team, but the strange thing was that the whole time I was there I was never known as John Skelton. I was always known as Jack Skelton, for reasons I can't tell you. I do know that quite often Johns are called Jack but I had never been called that before and Jack Skelton just stuck. I used to run in their sports day and win a prize or two, of course Peggy and the two boys used to come along and watch. I was also in the football team and you'll see from the photograph that I was the captain and we are holding some cup or other. I can't remember what cup it was but we were a fairly good footballing team. My progress was such that I was now on the staff and I enjoyed the responsibility of the position I was given.

A great team with me holding the cup

There was trouble at home and it was the health of Martin. He was severely asthmatic, he needed a lot of attention and not only that, he was not an outward going boy. Roland on the other hand was into all sorts of mischief, but Martin would rather be on his own in the back garden doing nothing really other than wandering about thinking inwardly. He looked like somebody who had just come out of a concentration camp, thin as a rake, you could see his chest bone through his skin. He really became quite a worry to both Peggy and myself and there was of course some interference from his grandmother who rather tended to think that I was a little hard on him in trying to toughen him up. I knew that something had to be done in order for him to survive in the world around him. When he got to the age of five he had to go to school. I can tell you that it was a problem, in as much that every day for the first three years he had to be taken to school and he cried. He never went in the playground, he went straight into his classroom where the head teacher would take him and from then onwards he would be under her control. She told us many years later she had never dealt with a child with this sort of complex. He needed careful attention because of his asthma, and he had all sorts of problems with things that he might eat that could close up his throat, particularly nuts. He had a terrible time when we were up in Shendish once when the bluebells were in full force and the smell of the bluebells actually knocked him right out. We had to rush him home, a doctor was called and he had to have an injection straight away to bring him back to normal. He was not an easy child to handle.

In those days of course when you got to the age of five or so everybody played out in the street. There were a lot of children, there were no cars and no problem of people being run over. The kids played football out in the street, but not Martin, he was content to stay in the back garden, almost on his own. Roland would be out there with the hustle and bustle. So Martin had to come under the supervision of a psychiatrist and the psychiatrist found him a very complicated sort of little boy. His instructions to us were that at six or seven years old he had to be sent out into the street to play with the other boys – open the door, take him out and do not let him come back in. It certainly brought tears and the whole thing was a nightmare for Peggy, her hair started to drop out in lumps and she was beside herself. However I was quite adamant that we should continue doing what the psychiatrist said, even though Martin came crying at the door to come back in. He was not allowed in until we said he could come in, he had to go out and play with the other children. Fortunately the school were understanding and they allowed Roland to go to school with him when he was four and a half instead of reaching the age of five. So Peggy did have to take them both at first but in the end Martin went with Roland and they would hold hands and go to school together. It was an extremely worrying time for us, difficult to know exactly what we should do. We knew that we had a child with severe asthma – when we were on holiday if a little wind blew on him then he would be coughing and spluttering and would have all sorts of problems. It was something which had to be overcome and how it was to be overcome was without doubt down to the perseverance of Martin himself. He had to realise that we could only guide him, but to overcome this particular problem was really something within himself.

Just before Martin went to school, I think he was perhaps three or four, we had an addition to the family, a dog – a mongrel, bought by Martin's grandmother who thought it might help him, and so we had this little puppy. It was like a little fox and that was the size that it grew to, about the size of a fox, same colour, same shape and really of the same intelligence. So the family is now mother, father, two sons and a dog.

How Rinty was named I really cannot recall, or who actually named him. Everybody in Hobbs Hill knew Rinty. It was a time when dogs used to go out of the house and roam, unlike today. There was no restriction such as dogs having to be put on a lead, there was no such thing as having to take a paper with you to clear up any mess that they made. I don't quite understand why, but it was the case that dogs were simply allowed to roam the streets on their own. Rinty grew up and his favourite place was down in the canal, he would run down, have a good swim and come back. Unfortunately sometimes he swam in the sort of muddy parts and it caused a little bit of a problem trying to clean him up. He was a lovely dog and extremely obedient, he did exactly what he was told and we never had a vet bill. He never had a tin of meat or anything like that bought for him. He just ate what we ate. When we made meals then he got part of that meal. He did used to like liver and quite often liver was bought for him, the only trouble being that when he had it he used to make terrible smells, so it was more of a luxury to him than something that he had regularly. He lived until he was seventeen.

The two boys were now attending Belswains Junior School. It was a new school and the headmaster's name was Mr Sully. He was a very good headmaster; he set up the parent-teacher association along with the schoolmistress of the infant side of the school and he asked me to be the secretary of the PTA. I was pleased and I accepted the position. It happened almost simultaneously with the chairman of the board of EAC approaching me and asking me if I would become the secretary of the Works Council. I had hardly ever seen him before, I knew him of course and I knew that he walked in and out of the works manager's office but he was not the sort of person you would normally come in contact with. He lived in a very large house in Leverstock Green. I used to pass by that house on my bicycle when I was going backwards and forwards to work. He would have his very large shiny car driving to St. Albans and back every day whereas I was riding on my Raleigh. However there it was, we all know that life isn't fair, it's not one of those things you have to worry about. In any case I always used to think to myself 'Well who was the happiest?' I knew in my mind who was.

In 1952, I think it was, I had a very big surprise at EAC. I was called into the Works Manager's office with the Personnel Manager and told that I was going to be made up to become Outside Work Controller. The current person was moving on to a more technical job and I was going to take his place. I nearly fell over I must say. It meant a nice large increase in my salary, and it meant that not only was I now a member of staff but I would also be entitled to an annual bonus according to the profits of the company. I had my own desk and my own teleprinter and telephone, and I was now Mr Jack Skelton. I was now a very young but senior member of the works management team. When I went home and told Peggy this she was highly delighted. It meant that we were now able to do a number of things that we couldn't do beforehand. It was a lot of responsibility, but I've never run away from that. I might have mentioned that I often had more confidence than ability and I think that came to the fore then. I was not in any way, shape or form frightened of the job.

It meant that we were able to buy things, do more things to the house, we had carpets on the floor and we always had our holidays. We even bought a fridge which was a little above what most households had at that time. After I'd been doing the job for about a year I would think, unfortunately I broke my leg playing football for EAC. I knew it was broken, I heard the click, I felt the pain. The ambulance came on and I was whisked off to hospital. They fixed the leg and put it in plaster. I'm not sure how Peggy found out, I really don't know, just that she did turn up to the hospital in St Albans.

It was a bit of a blow because I'd only been doing the outside work controller job for possibly a year and things seemed to be going reasonably well. Now I was off with this broken leg. I was quite friendly with the personnel manager and after I was away for some two or three weeks or so, something like that, he came to see me and made arrangements that he would come and pick me up three days a week so that I could keep in touch with what was going on. Charlie Kingston came to the house and of course he met my wife and we were quite friendly, and that friendship lasted all the time that I was actually at EAC.

We were now coming up to the Coronation of 1953. King George VI had died the year before and his daughter Elizabeth was coming to the throne. There were massive celebrations and flags and all sorts, the usual sort of celebrations for such an occasion, and we decided to get a television set, there were only two sets in the road. In those days you didn't buy television sets, you rented them, and they had very small screens. We also rented a washing machine – we weren't what one would call absolutely flush with money but we were very comfortable. Peggy herself had five or six pupils who used to come to the house to learn the piano so she was also a contributor to the weekly income. On the day of the Coronation there was a fancy dress parade at the school. I really can't remember what our two boys went as, but they would have been dressed up – we were the sort of people who entered into all of those sorts of activities. Peggy has always said that she was the only person in the room who didn't actually see the Coronation because she was busy making cups of tea and sandwiches etc. for other people. So it was her television set but it was crowded out with a lot of other people. It was a fun day, we enjoyed it, the weather was good and with all the flags and all the commotion going on it was just one of those days which people simply do not forget.

I think it was towards the end of 1954 when the job of outside work controller changed considerably from being an administrative post and one which needed a lot of planning and forethought to a more technical aspect. Electronic or electrical engineering came more into the type of decisions that I was having to make and I was lost, there was no question about that, it played on my mind. I even went on a course at the college to try and get some sort of technical understanding of what people were talking about, but I have never been a person who has been able to get to grips with things of a technical nature. So although nobody at home noticed any difference I was thinking about it all the time and I wasn't happy with what I was doing, partly because I was not in control.

When you get to the stage where you feel you're not in control of things then life becomes quite difficult. I hadn't talked to Peggy or anybody about how I was feeling, I just went to work and came home. I've never been the sort of person who's brought my work or worries home, I've always tended to sort them out myself and do the best that I could. But one day I went to work and as I was cycling there I thought to myself, 'Well, I'm going to give this up.' When the personnel manager came in I went into his office, as I've said before we were quite friendly and I had quite a longish chat with him where I said I didn't want any fuss, I just wanted to leave. In actual fact what I wanted to do was to leave there and then and not have to say goodbye to these people who had been good to me. I'd made lots of friends but I simply wanted to go. He understood perfectly and he took me down to the wages office, my wages were all done up, my holiday money and all sorts of things which you get when you're leaving employment.

We shook hands and I went home. He obviously went back and had to talk to the works manager and the team. What he said I've really no idea and what other people thought, again I only heard – once or twice people were surprised that Jack Skelton had left. Of course I now had to cycle home, not quite knowing what I was going to say when I arrived but it had to be done. I went in the front door and Peggy was upstairs. I called up and she was surprised to see me. I went upstairs, we were on the landing and I told her what had happened, that I had got close to a breakdown and that there was only one thing for me to do and that was to leave. There was no argument, no, nothing at all, we didn't say very much at all really. We went into the bedroom, we undressed until we were absolutely naked, we got into bed, we fell into each other's arms, both in tears, and that's where we stayed for the rest of the morning. We got up and had lunch with the boys when they came home from school, they went back to school and we went back to bed. Peggy was always confident that I would be able to sort things out and that's how we spoke, 'We'll work it out.' 'Well I know we will, you've always done it in the past and that's what will happen in the future.'

We were fortunate that we did have some savings and I had the holiday money etc. I told Peggy that I was quite confident I would get another job. I wasn't the sort of person who would be sitting around waiting for somebody to employ me; I would be out there trying to get some sort of employment. I must admit that we were both of us in a daze but I can tell you once again what a very special person Peggy was, because she had total faith, she gave me confidence that I would be able to sort things out and that in the end it would all turn out to be OK. So I was finished with EAC and there was another future to look forward to, whatever that future was going to be.

The following two or three days are quite hazy in my mind. I'm not sure whether Peggy or I were actually living on the planet, we were in such a daze. I know that I did a lot of gardening because we had a large garden. We had a lot of soft fruit, blackcurrant, redcurrants, gooseberries etc. I used to grow dahlias and I was pretty good with them, and of course the normal vegetable patch, and then at the top of the garden was the sort of lawn where the children played and there were roses which used to go over a trellised archway. The garden looked nice, a lot of people did comment on how nice we kept it. So during that first week I was able to relax my mind. I didn't actually look for employment during that time, I was just coming to terms with what was going to happen in the future.

9

Peggy and I were still very much in love with each other, we enjoyed each other's company, we were not despondent in any shape or form; anybody who knows us will know that it wasn't a depressed house at all, we just carried on. We both knew that the tide would turn again and that something would turn up. The next week I had to start looking for a job through the labour exchange and through reading adverts in the paper. Some that I wrote to didn't reply, but I came across an advert for a company which sold cash registers to shopkeepers and you didn't need to have your own car or transport. It was a job where you went by public transport, but you were cold calling, going into towns like Watford or St Albans or Hemel and calling on shopkeepers trying to sell them a cash register. I applied for the job and I got it. I can't tell you what the salary was or what commission I was being paid, really that's quite gone from my memory. But there it is, I was now a salesman trying to sell cash registers to, well in the main, small shopkeepers.

I can't say that it was a job which appealed to me and I can't say it had a future. I knew that this was a stopgap, but I did it. I can't remember the length of time I did the job but I did well and I earned money. I think the boss's name was Mr Downton. He was pleased with me and he used to pass on any sort of leads to me because he rather felt that I would make the sales. You see then the company was called the Gross Cash Register company; they were a small company and they were in competition with the big, national cash register company whose products I would think that the majority of the shopkeepers had. That didn't deter me. I went about and I did lots of calling. I was not uneasy when I got into a shop to talk to the proprietor etc. It made a nice income and we were able to carry on doing what we normally did. Towards the end of the time that I was with Gross I started to have an urge to take lessons to drive a motorcar. I thought that I was now in a position that, if I was going to stay in the game of selling, a car would be an enormous advantage to me and so I started to have lessons.

However I was starting to think that I really wasn't getting anywhere. I was employed, I was earning money that we could live on without too much bother or fuss, but I wasn't making any real headway. I always said that I'd like to be my own boss, to make my own decisions and to live by those decisions. I came across a man who was a greengrocer in Hemel Hempstead and we talked about the sort of living that a greengrocery shop could give you. Hemel was still a growing town and the houses were being built very much faster than the shopping centres, so people bought stuff at the door and I knew traders had regular customers. It got into my head that perhaps I should buy a van and get in contract with a wholesale greengrocer. I picked up this information from the guy who had the greengrocery shop in the High Street, he was pointing me in the right direction. Of course in the beginning the whole thing seemed to be crazy – I was going to give up the job I was doing, buy a van, buy some greengrocery at wholesale prices, knock on people's doors, and try and sell the greengrocery on a regular basis. Crazy, of course, but when I talked to Peggy about it, although she thought I was going a little mad, but once again she said to me, 'I know you'll sort something out and I know what you'll do, you'll make some sort of success of it.' Once again there was no argument about what the hell are you doing that for? And how do you think we are going to live? Nothing, nothing about that at all, she just allowed me to ponder, and eventually that is exactly what happened. I left Gross Cash Registers and I had started the preparation to be a greengrocer.

What I had to do was get permission from the council that I could actually store a stock of greengrocery in the shed and in part of the house. They agreed that as long as I didn't sell from the house and as long as I did no trading whatsoever from the house, it was perfectly all right. I had to purchase a van and I was still without a driving licence, although I was still having lessons and hoping that I would eventually pass. I just had to wait and jump that hurdle when it came. I had to have portable shelves put in the van and a set of scales to weigh the fruit etc. It was all a bit of a mystery to me but I'd made up my mind and this was the way that we were going to go. Of course Peggy's mother was extremely upset, and she made some rather nasty sort of comments. She said she didn't know that her daughter was eventually going to be married to a street hawker, which I could understand. I laughed it off, and I think I said once, 'You'll have to remember that big oak trees actually start from a little acorn, and that's where we'll be, we'll be that little acorn which will grow to a large oak tree'.

Ten days before my driving test a friend's father said he that would come with me to begin with, because he did have a driving licence. I gave him a small payment and he got free greengrocery. I think he wanted something to do during the day and he was quite good company while I was driving but he took no part in the selling at all. I had to visit a wholesale greengrocery in Watford and a system of payment had to be worked out, then so as far as I could make out everything was ready for the off. Can you imagine how my heart beat as I drove away that very first day and knocked at that very first door? I knew it would be hard work but I was determined and was certainly not afraid of working hard. My driving test was now so important and on that day I was more than nervous, I would say petrified. I passed first time. Hooray! I was now able to relax.

After a week or so it was difficult to determine exactly what was going to happen. Once again Peggy came up trumps by saying that she would come with me on some days, and do you know she liked working and talking to customers and they really liked her. We were on our way. It looked as though we were going to be able make something of our future. We started to make some money despite repairs to the van and the weather not always being helpful. It's surprising how quickly you get to like being outside. It was a strange feeling really that when it was pouring with rain and I was out there in it I didn't mind, because it would mean that there were more people indoors and so more people came to the van. We were starting to have regular customers that we would call on a couple of times or so a week, and then other people would come out from their houses when they saw the van. As the time went by people not only became customers but friends as well, people we socialised with over a good number of years and we kept in contact with those people for a very long time.

At the top of Hobbs Hill Road they built four shops, and one of them was to be a greengrocer's shop. The guy who came from Hemel, who actually got me started and we had kept in touch, took over the lease of that shop. After I'd been trading for about a year and a half he asked me if I'd like to take over the lease and after discussions with the council, that is exactly what I did. I became a shop keeper, I kept my best customers that I had on the round and I also carried on with calling on customers week by week. We were doing well and once again Peggy got on well with customers and it settled us into a routine. Unfortunately we had problems over a Christmas period because of course we had to spend time with Peggy's mother and father. What we both liked to do was to join the traditional party at my mother's house which always had a large family gathering. I can tell you that the party went on through Christmas day, Christmas night and well into Boxing day with my brothers and sisters all enjoying a great time. When we get together these days, we always talk about those Christmas parties at 310 Parsloes Avenue. My mother was known as Granny Murray right up to a very old age. She was able to sing and dance with the rest of us and I think I must have got my energy from her.

Martin was doing much better at school, he worked very hard and his teachers were pleased with his progress, but he did not want anything to do with greengrocery whereas Roland became involved on the rounds. He loved meeting people and they liked him. Because we were selling more I was able to take the van to Brentford market and buy stuff somewhat cheaper than I was able to do from the wholesaler. The stories regarding Christmas trees in the car and in the van are absolutely legendary. Roland particularly liked the breakfast that Doris used to dish up during those cold, dark, early mornings which made everything worthwhile and exciting.

A subject that used to come up regularly was Peggy's desire to have a little baby girl. Of course it was out of the question, her getting pregnant, and so the question of fostering was talked about quite a lot. Before anything could be done the boys had to come in and be consulted when we were discussing what we wanted to do. It meant a great deal to them that there would be someone else and they would have to give up their separate rooms – we had a three bedroom house which meant they would have to sleep together in one room. Peggy and I had to admire the way the boys were happy with this situation and so we decided to go forth and make the first move to become foster parents. By now I had purchased a car and we had our holidays, we had our days away etc. I would not say that there weren't any troubles because Martin was still an asthmatic and had to be tended with some care, but as a family we were extremely happy. Then the social services got in touch. Although they knew that we were only wanting a baby girl they came with the story that there were two half-sisters. The courts had taken away the parental rights from the mother, and at the moment the sisters were being fostered by a family who were only going to have them for a week. If we didn't take them they were going to go into a children's home within a day or two. A very difficult decision. In actual fact there were three sisters, or three half-sisters, one half-sister was going to stay with the grandmother who was going to look after the eldest one and the other two were going into a children's home. Once again it was a family discussion, the family would go from two to four, and we didn't know much of the girls' upbringing.

The day that they came, the social worker brought them to the door and into the hall. I'm afraid that there were two desperately unhappy children. Jackie was ten months old and Lesley was two and a quarter. It was 17 February 1957. Their clothes were dirty, they had sores on their faces, bedraggled, looking in absolute desperation towards us. We looked at each other and thought to ourselves well, what have we done here? Peggy has always said that the ice was broken when Lesley put her hand into Peggy's hand and said, 'So you're my new Mummie then?' There were tears, but from that moment onwards until this day they became our daughters and sisters to our two boys. Jackie is now fifty-seven and Lesley is now fifty-nine.

The very next day Peggy had to take the two girls to the doctor – apparently it was the rules of social services that they had to be seen by a doctor in the state in which they arrived with us. It was an extremely embarrassing time for Peggy to take these two dishevelled children into the waiting room while she was quite nicely dressed as she always was. Unfortunately Lesley was prone to swearing; all sorts of 'bugger' and 'bloody' and 'shit' came from her mouth quite regularly. I guessed she had heard those words constantly in her upbringing. Things changed almost immediately when our friends and neighbours found out what we were doing, and clothes, dolls, toys, dolls houses all sorts of things came from these people. It was incredible the way in which people gathered round us and hoped we would make a success it. The girls were a bit bewildered but there it is, they settled in. It wasn't an easy time but it wasn't as difficult as you might imagine. They were with us and we were going to be their mum and dad for the rest of their lives.

I know that throughout this book I have written many times about what a special person Peggy was, and I'm not apologising for that in any shape or form. I'd just like people to ponder when they read it, on what happened at the time that Jackie and Lesley came to us. Here we were, a family who were not rich but we were comfortably well off, had a nice lifestyle, certainly not too many money worries. People would probably say, 'Well what a nice family. You've got a boy who is now getting on to eleven and one who is nine, and you're going to take on these two girls, these two babies, one ten months and the other two and a quarter? Not knowing what is ahead of you?' Well, what would you do? Only a special person would take on that responsibility knowing that life was going to be very different. From time to time it was difficult but happy. Peggy had a lot of love to give, we both did.

10

Martin passed the eleven plus examination and went on to be a pupil at Apsley Grammar School. As a result everything that he wore had to be not only clean and tidy but in correct order, his socks were always pulled up to the correct level, his hat was always put on perfectly straight and his tie was always in position. Unlike Roland, whose socks were always around his shoes. Roland was just one of those people who always looked as though he was ready to have a bath as opposed to looking clean and tidy. On a school trip once he took a case with his change of clothing in it and when he came back he opened the case and nothing had changed – he had worn the same clothes the whole week. Furthermore he'd looked out of the train windows while the train was going through tunnels and his face was as black as the ace of spades.

Both Martin and Roland were very keen on football, they were totally different players in as much that Martin was extremely timid in his approach although as the years went on he certainly grew out of that. He became quite a ferocious player as many of the opponents that he played against later on in life will attest. On the other hand Roland was fortunate in as much that he could kick quite easily and very hard and certainly with good direction, with both feet. He didn't have to think about whether he should kick with his left foot or his right foot, whichever one it came to he was able to use, which is a big asset. He was a little cumbersome and slow, but for all of that he scored many goals while playing football with either foot. At the grammar school Martin was always reserve for the first team but he always turned up with his perfect kit in his case. The sports master, Mr Parslow, said to me that he just had to play him sometimes because of his enthusiasm, and of course he was not wrong because Martin then became a regular player with Apsley Grammar first team.

I became Chairman of Bennetts End community centre, so I was quite a busy person but I did my share with Peggy bringing up the two girls, which was quite demanding. Friends and neighbours and all sorts of people turned up trumps in assisting us with having four children to look after. I know Peggy would have been somewhat annoyed with the report that I originally read from social services in regard to us fostering the two girls. It said in one part: 'It was a very nice house, a very warm family and it had nice furniture, etc. However it always seemed to be untidy with a haphazard routine.' I knew then that the writer could never have dealt with four children who could easily leave everything all over the place.

Jackie and Lesley settled in very well, they loved Rinty and Rinty loved playing around with them, he was very good with children. We all fitted in together, it was a very close happy family. Fortunately we were doing very well in the shop. I had purchased a car which meant that we went much further afield and we spent our time as a family. When Jackie was about three or four she became a little insecure and she had to come into our bed. On many occasions after she'd woken up in the night she had to sleep on my side. I was facing her and we were almost nose to nose, but what I mustn't do was to breathe on her. How it was possible to do that I can't tell you but I was really asked to do the impossible. She did that on many occasions but of course, with both Lesley and Jackie, you had to remember that they were subjected to a not very nice upbringing in the part of their lives, so nothing that either of them did really caused us a great deal of concern.

Roland sat his eleven plus but unfortunately he just failed. Mr Sully his headmaster spoke on his behalf to the head of Apsley Grammar School, who knew Martin, and he agreed to take Roland into Apsley Grammar School after two years in the comprehensive school, which was actually next door. He said that he would take him on the understanding that he did well in those first examinations, which he did, and he then changed from Bennetts End Comprehensive to Apsley Grammar School so that the boys were both going to the same school.

I bought a film camera with a projector and a screen to film part of our family holidays which we had always had every year. This equipment was to take the place of the photographs. It was of course a very old camera; if it had no battery what you had to was wind it up and the roll of film that you put into it just lasted four minutes. In all I think I must have some twenty or more films and some years ago I had about fourteen put into one video. We used to go to Clintonville quite often for our seaside holiday and these films show Peggy with her love of cream cakes, and also her getting into the water with children. She loved being in the water with them, she couldn't swim herself but she enjoyed the play that took place. Martin always liked his friend Vic Marino to come along with us and so we had an extra child to look after although the boys more or less looked after themselves. Peggy's cousin Joan used to come from Ramsgate with her husband and her children and play the games and go into the water with us. The highlight of our day would be the walk in which we always stopped at the cream shop that also sold shellfish. That's where Roland and I got the taste for eating whelks; we still do and we still use the phrase 'black as the ace of spades but as sweet as a nut', which is how we'd describe the whelks after we'd eaten them. I often get these videos out to watch how happy we all were at the time, and I switch it off, have a few tears and then go to bed.

The happy family on holiday

About that time I was invited to be the chairman of Hemel Hempstead Football Club. Goodness I certainly had a few part time jobs to attend to, but I accepted and the team did very well indeed. Roland enjoyed himself while I was chairman. He used to cut the grass and I think what he enjoyed most of all was driving the fairly large motor mower. I think he thought he was driving around Silverstone. He was a great help to the guy who used to keep the ground in good condition. While I was there I was also voted onto the Herts FA council and I was also the delegate for the Athenian League administration council.

As the delegate for the Athenian League I was approached by the delegate for Finchley football club who wanted someone other than himself to speak on behalf of Wingate football club. Both of these clubs were sort of Jewish clubs, and they were attached to each other. He asked if I would speak in order for Wingate football club to join the Athenian league as there was one place available at that particular time. He would second the proposal. I spoke for them and they were invited into the league, and from that moment onwards, for several years, both Peggy and I were invited to Wingate football club's annual dinner and dance. It was always held at a very posh London venue, I feel sure it was the Dorchester, if it wasn't it was somewhere of that stature. Anyway we were wined and dined and spoilt on those evenings and made to feel very special.

John on left, Peggy on right. Ready for the dance

Being a representative of the Herts FA council I was asked to go to many of the local football clubs annual dinner and dances and I became quite well known as an after dinner speaker. Quite frequently in my speech I would say that the audience that night were lucky because there was a young lady with them who was a world champion. The audience would wonder who it was. I would then say, 'She happens to be sitting next to me and she is World Champion Shusher. She got the title due to the number of times she has said, "Shush John, you're talking too much," or "Shush John, you're drinking too much".' It always went down well.

I would say I guess that I was a busy man but with a very busy social life too. About that time a nightclub opened in Luton called Caesar's Palace. On a Saturday night Peggy and I and our friends would go there and we saw a number of top-class artists. Such people as Tom Jones, Shirley Bassey, Tommy Cooper, Matt Monro and many others. We were very happy to go there with our friends, we'd come back and we'd always have a little party. Our social life

90

was almost as hectic as our working lives, so I guess we just must have had a great deal of energy. During the next few years with our friends we went to Ascot Ladies Day every year, we also went to the Cheltenham national hunt festival. Each year I went with a friend named Charlie who lived in Leverstock Green to the Derby, I can't remember his surname. I'd met him on a Derby day. We always went to the Derby together. On a Friday night I went to Hendon dogs and Roland came with me – he enjoyed every minute of cutting up old losing tickets etc. He got to know that one and four reverse sometimes got us out of any trouble we might be in. I also served on the committee for the Hemel Hempstead Carnivals held every year in August, don't ask me how I fitted all of these jobs in I really can't tell you. A year or two ago I was talking to Lesley and she said to me that all she can remember of those times really was how I was always working so hard on something or another: 'You never seemed to sit down and just do nothing.' She was probably quite right; I always had a tremendous amount of energy and although I haven't got that same amount of energy now, I guess for an eighty-nine-year-old I would be considered to be someone who is not yet too decrepit.

We had some problems with Lesley at Belswains School, although she was doing very well with her violin lessons. Peggy helped of course by accompanying her at her practice time and in fact she won the St. Cecelia trophy given to the best musician at the school. She went on from there to win a scholarship to the Royal Academy of Music just before she was thirteen. Both Peggy and Lesley went to violin lessons with a professor from the Royal Academy. Jackie on the other hand liked her dancing and all the fun that went with that and had weekly dancing lessons. She was in fact a very popular young girl with both boys and girls. When she got older she served in the shop on Saturdays and she was very popular with the customers, they liked her very much indeed. Lesley was quite different, she had one or two friends and was more withdrawn than Jackie.

Both Lesley and Jackie went to Adeyfield School, partly because they specialised in secretarial courses and we thought that was the way they should go. However I'm afraid neither took schooling very seriously, it was more like fun and games with Jackie and we were never at all certain that Lesley actually turned up for her lessons. However everyone is different and we did not get into any serious disagreements over exactly what they were doing. I don't know that Jackie did her very best at school, she certainly didn't do as well as she was capable of doing but her school days were certainly fun. Roland was a great help with the greengrocery business, both with the shop and the van. The customers liked him and he enjoyed the hustle and bustle of Brentford market and all the banter that we had with our customers. The customers certainly liked him too and when he was away at college, which was some time later, they always asked where he was.

Two More Trophies For Bennetts End

COUNTY Youth champions Bennetts End have added two more trophies to their collection. On Thursday evening last week at Watford they won the Watford Medal Competition for the first time in their history with a 4—0 victory over South Oxhey, and on Monday evening they collected the West Herts Minor Cup for the fourth time by defeating Woodside 5—3 at Kings Langley.

South Oxhey were hardly in the picture and fell behind in the 22nd minute when Keith WILLIAMS converted a pass from Tony Roe. Eight minutes later, Williams return the compliment for ROE to score.

John WALLACE increased the lead from close-range in the 67th minute before ROE completed the tally 29 minutes after the break with the best goal of the match. He let loose a pile-driver from 25 yards which curled into the top corner of the net giving the South Oxhey keeper no chance to save.

After leading 2—1 at half-time, Bennetts End surged into a 5—1 lead against Woodside on Monday night, but fell away towards the end and conceded a couple of late goals.

Bennetts End's scorers were Wallace (2), Rogers (2) and Williams.

Scouts from Wealdstone and Fulham watched the match and showed interest in left-back Grierson and left-half Vic Marino.

17-YEAR-OLD MARTIN SAVES HEMPSTEAD

HERTFORD RES. 2; HEMEL HEMPSTEAD TOWN RES. 1

MARTIN SKELTON, Bennetts End's 17-year-old keeper, came to the rescue of Hemel Hempstead Town on Friday evening and played a big part in restricting formidable Hertford to a one-goal lead in the first leg for the Delphian League's Reserve championship

Just before players and officials left for Hertford, reserve keeper Peter Smith called off with a broken nose and it was too late to contact Kevin O'Brien so in stepped Martin—son of club chairman John Skelton. It was a tough "blooding" for the Bennetts End youngster but he came through with flying colours. True, there were times when his lack of experience caused dangerous situations, but he soon settled down and undoubtedly saved a second half drubbing when Hertford really piled on the pressure.

Ten minutes after the start, Skelton dived full-length to tip a drive by right-half Sneddon round a post, but shortly afterwards he dropped the ball during a goal-mouth melee. Inside-left Miller snapped up the chance and netted but the referee ruled that the Hempstead keeper had been fouled.

Although his midfield play was quite good, Hempstead's attack was disjointed and the only worthwhile effort in the first period came from right-half Laing, who was only inches wide with a free-kick.

MARTIN SKELTON

TWO BEHIND

Hertford took the lead in the 30th minute when inside-left MILLER headed in a left-wing cross and left-half PELLING put the side further ahead 12 minutes after the break with a fierce drive which Skelton just failed to reach.

At this stage, Hempstead fell away and were penned back by a lively Hertford side which included several senior team players. But somehow the defence held out and after a serious of breakaway efforts, Keith HILL cracked in a great left-footed drive from the edge of the box.

Last night Hempstead received Hertford in the second leg.

Hemel Hempstead: Skelton; Marsden, Dorman; Laing, Fenton, Kelly; Johnson, Sykes, Hill, Lewis, Hume.

I had a phone call from Les Hall who was the manager of Hemel Hempstead football club to tell me that the reserve team game against Hertford town was without a goalkeeper. He knew that Martin played in that position and wondered if he would be available. We pulled out all the stops and Martin, with me and his granddad, turned up for this game. He had a blinder, just read the report and make up your own mind. It was the start of his footballing career. He captained Herts public school and grammar school teams, not as a goalkeeper but as a ferocious forward. Strangely enough a year or so later Roland also captained the same side, football was obviously in their blood. In 1966 I went to both semi-finals of the World Cup in 1966 and I also had tickets to be at the actual final, in which of course we beat Germany. I had a banner in the shop window to say that we would win the cup and sure enough we did. Peggy and I and two friends went into London that evening to the Café Royale and celebrated, what a night! I do not recall how we got home, all I know is that it was an evening that was talked about many times over the years.

Chairman: D. R. HOWELLS, Esq.   President: R. DOYLE, Esq.   Vice-Chairman: W. A. ISON, Esq.
Vice-President: A. TERRY, Esq.
Hon. Gen. Sec. and Treasurer (Social):
R. F. HAMBLIN, 27 Sawyers Way, Hemel Hempstead, Herts.
Hemel Hempstead 50622

Hemel Hempstead Football & Sports Club

Formerly APSLEY FOOTBALL CLUB — Founded 1885
Club Colours—ALL RED
Ground—VAUXHALL ROAD, HEMEL HEMPSTEAD, HERTS.
Telephone: HEMEL HEMPSTEAD 2081. (Board Room 4532)

Members of
THE ATHENIAN LEAGUE
Affiliated to the Herts. F.A.

Associate Members of
THE FOOTBALL
ASSOCIATION

Date— 8th. Nov: 1972.

Please reply to—
F.H.Hayward.

Football Section
Hon. Secretary:
F. H. HAYWARD,
13 Seymour Crescent,
Hemel Hempstead, Herts.
Hemel Hempstead 2819
(Private)
Hemel Hempstead 4461/2/3
(Business)

Hon. Press Secretary:
F. H. HAYWARD,
13 Seymour Crescent,
Hemel Hempstead, Herts.
Hemel Hempstead 2819
(Private)
Hemel Hempstead 4461/2/3
(Business)

Hon. Match Secretary:
W. McGRAE,
209 Fletcher Way,
Hemel Hempstead, Herts.
Hemel Hempstead 51503

Assistant Hon. Match
Secretary:
K. ELDRIDGE,
85 Sawyers Way,
Hemel Hempstead, Herts.
Hemel Hempstead 55695

Hon. Treasurer:
R. DOYLE,
7 Patmore Link Road,
H.   Hempstead, Herts.

Team Manager:
D. PRICE,
10 Coverdale,
Hemel Hempstead, Herts.
Hemel Hempstead 50919

Martin Skelton,
43, Alexandra Road,
Kings Langley,
Herts.

Dear Martin,

I was naturally very disappointed to receive your resignation last Saturday. On the other hand I suppose I can understand your frustration knowing that we have two good goalkeepers, only one of which is able to retain his place in the first eleven.

I would like to thank you, on behalf of all the Officers past and present, and all those other people who have received an awful lot of pleasure in watching you perform between the sticks.

I wish you well at Chesham and hope that your journey was necessary.

Please convey my very best wishes to Ann, I hope that your two children are doing well.

Good Luck Martin,
Yours sincerely,

F.H.Hayward,
Hon. Secretary, Football Section.

P.S. Please don't forget to hand your bag to Johnny Wallace,
or someone

I must now go back to January 1965 when the great Sir Winston Churchill died. It was a day of deep mourning for this great man from the whole of the population. I well remember his speeches, the most famous of course when we were in our darkest days; the Blitz, Dunkirk and the inevitable thought that we were about to be invaded. Along with many thousands of other people, Roland and I went to see his lying in state in Westminster Abbey. We were both completely overwhelmed by the experience. We joined the queue half way over London Bridge, and I'm not sure how long we waited but we were both of the same mind that it was an occasion that we would not have wanted to miss.

Sir Winston Churchill lying in state

Martin was coming up to leaving school and he had interviews with a bank manager and also with the manager of McAlpines, the building company, for a position in the computer department. He chose the computer department and he has never looked back from that position. Roland had decided to leave school to go to Borough Road College to be a sports and maths teacher. I resigned as chairman of Hemel Hempstead football club, I think around 1968 or 1969, I must say under somewhat of a cloud but that is a story for another time. It meant that I was no longer involved in any shape or form with football.

11

The business was in decline due to Hemel Hempstead growing as a town, leading to more public transport, more shops and the opening of super-markets etc. It needed a great deal more of my attention and time. Peggy's father, who had been in poor health for some time, died in 1971. At that time Peggy's mother and father were living in the flat above the shop and I knew that Peggy felt rightly or wrongly that her mother would not be able to cope on her own. It was a difficult decision for me but I knew what it meant to Peggy and so I agreed that she should live with us. From that moment onwards Peggy looked after her, hand and foot, for the next seven years. Just before granddad's death I had to make a decision about extra income and I saw an advert in the paper for evening debt collectors for GUS who were the owners of Cavendish, Woodhouse and Times Furnishing Company. I applied and got the part time job. Once again I applied myself to the job and was successful and strangely enough I had a good reception when I got into conversation with the people who were getting into arrears with their account. I was never heavy handed and I left the people with the sense that I was trying to help them as opposed to beat them about the head.

The next bombshell that Peggy and I had to deal with was that Lesley, who was getting on for eighteen and was still at school, became pregnant. We found out about this when she put a note under her pillow. She used to keep quite a few odds and ends under her pillow, and she knew that Peggy would be making the bed and was bound to see that note in the morning telling her, well both of us of course, that she was pregnant. We were absolutely dumbfounded. She wasn't the sort of young girl who was flirty or going about at dances or things like that, she was most probably the last person in the world that you would think would become pregnant. However she was pregnant. Of course when she came home there were tears and long discussions as to what should be done or how we should go about it but we both told her that whatever happened we would help with looking after the child. The father first of all would not accept the fact that he was the father but he had tests and it was found that he was the father. Not that he ever fathered in the way you would imagine, he never made any contribution towards the upkeep of the child and never really saw his child. So there we were with another child coming into the family. We had to turn our dining room into another bedroom and so at that time we actually did have four bedrooms as opposed to three.

I'm afraid that at this moment in time I'm getting things a little bit out of sequence but you'll forgive me for this because I haven't a diary and therefore I have to rely on sometimes other people and my own memory as to a sequence of events, and lots of things are happening in our house around about those particular few years.

Martin was courting. He met Ann and they became engaged, and then they were married on 9 September 1967. Lesley and Jackie were their bridesmaids. Ann was an extremely attractive girl and very photogenic. Her wedding photographs with Martin and the whole set up were absolutely magnificent. Something unfortunate happened though, in as much that we had the shop at that time, and a lady customer came in and told us that she would decorate the church for the wedding. She had heard the banns being called for Ann in Leverstock Green church and she said that she was a professional flower arranger and if we provided the flowers she would go into the hedgerow and get the bracken and all that type of thing which went with flower decorations. So it all went along and she came and showed us what she'd taken from the hedge row and I bought the flowers from the wholesale market. I can't remember what they were but I know that they were very good flowers and there were plenty of them. When we arrived at the church on the day there were just two vases of half dead daffodils! I had told my friend whose daughter was getting married immediately after Martin and Ann not to worry about the church decoration because I'd taken great care of that. What a disappointment, what a surprise.

However, on the Monday morning the customer came into the shop and said did we like the decoration she'd done? She apologised for the fact that she wasn't able to get to the wedding itself but she said that the church looked very nice. We had to tell her that there was no decoration at all in the church where the wedding took place. She had decorated the wrong church. She was absolutely flabbergasted. I can tell you that she apologised and left, and do you know that we never saw her in our shop again.

We celebrated Martin and Ann's first wedding anniversary at Caesar's Palace, the nightclub in Luton. They loved a particular song sung by Tony Bennett, 'I left my heart in San Francisco', and unbeknown to me Martin had asked for it to be played and for an announcement to be made about the anniversary celebrations. I don't really know how this happened, but when the band struck up I started to dance with Ann as the MC was giving out the news People started to clap, thinking that I was the husband! What confusion and embarrassment there was when Martin came onto the floor to sort the whole matter out. That is a story that is told many times at family parties etc.

Roland was now at Borough Road College and there he met Rosalyn Curly. She was always known to us as Roz, and she became an item with Roland. She came from a very staunch Roman Catholic background, and her mother and father and family were not too pleased that she became attached to Roland. This became a little worse as wedding plans were drawn up and in fact she was unwelcome at her home and had to stay with us during term breaks, and so we got to know her very well. When the wedding plans were finalised, Roz's parents had nothing to do with it, in fact right up until the last minute they weren't actually coming to the wedding. In fact a few days before the wedding they did say that they would be coming with two or three of Roz's' relatives, and they did actually come to the wedding. Roz went to the church from a friend's house. She got ready there and travelled to the church from this house. The cost of the wedding and the honeymoon had to be borne by Peggy and me, and in fact Roland took my car for the week. I think they went camping for the week in France somewhere. We got to know both Ann and Roz very well, they were almost like daughters to us, certainly more than just ordinary in-laws. They enjoyed our family parties, and all seemed to be going very well at the time.

I do have to tell you about when we lost Rinty, which happened before either of the boys got married. During the day Roland was in bed because he was working night shifts, I think it was at Kodak, while he was at college and so he was sleeping during the day. Now Rinty never went upstairs, he was a very obedient dog but on this occasion there was a violent storm and for some reason or another he went up into Roland's bedroom and he had a stroke. I don't think the vet was called to put him down, I think he actually died there and then. What a tragedy for us all, for the family. We all loved that dog – he was never any trouble and he really was one of the family.

I think I've said before that school for Jackie was more fun and games than actual studying. She was a very popular girl with her numerous friends and Saturday night dances and discos, I suppose they would be called in those days, were the feature of her whole week. We got to the stage where on a Saturday night, or at least by twelve o'clock or one o'clock in the morning, I would get a phone call to say she was sorry but the last bus didn't turn up and could I come and collect her from wherever she was? She could be as far afield as Welwyn Garden City and places like that so I was a fairly regular taxi driver. I know that Roland said on many occasions that he was never able to avail himself of the taxi because it was always booked so frequently by Jackie, but it was better for me to go and pick her and her friends up, all crammed into the car, as opposed to them being stranded out somewhere and unable to get back. For Jackie, life was all about having fun.

I realise that so far in the story I've mostly referred to Peggy as 'Peggy'. Of course that was her name, but she was always known to the family, to the children, even to her friends and to me and to her close relatives as 'Mummie'. Of course she was not my mother, she was my beloved wife, but from now onwards when you read the word Mummie you will know that I am referring to her. Her proper name was Evelyn, she was actually Evelyn Peggy Skelton, but she was always known as Peggy and in the family as Mummie.

I had now been a part time debt collector for about a year and I found that there were many flaws in the system. Of course the company was not computerised at that time and the head clerks were responsible for the debt in their particular branch using manual ledgers and really that put a great responsibility on their shoulders. I spoke to Harold Culpin, who was the supervisor in charge of me and the forty shops in the region, and he suggested that I write to the finance director about what I saw as the inefficiencies in controlling the bad debt situation. The finance director was a man named Tom Bentley and he called me up into his office in Nottingham. He told me he thought that I was doing extremely well and that Harold Culpin had spoken well of me and could see that in the two or three branches that I covered there had been considerable improvement. He offered me a full time job. I was really quite taken aback because he was offering me a very nice salary, a company van to travel about with, not a company car at that particular time, and I would be in charge of the eight other part time debt collectors throughout the region. Not only that, I would also be expected to go into the branches and talk to the head clerks in order to try and improve their debt situation which was not very good at that time. It would mean that I would have some evening work of course, to do with training the debt collectors, and that would mean that I would be away some nights. The regions went from Lowestoft and Great Yarmouth, Cambridge over to Oxford and all sorts of places that would have been difficult to get back from. I would be paid some very good expenses, the hotel fees were also covered and another small perk was that £5 could be put on my expenses sheet for drinks at the hotel if I had to stay there overnight.

The job attracted me very much and I accepted the whole situation. I obviously had to come back and speak to Mummie about what was going to happen, but she was very pleased and said, 'Well you know what you're doing John, and we just have to go along with that, I'm sure that we will come through as we always have done.' We had to have more help in the shop. We already had a cleaner who came in two days a week and someone else who did the washing for us, and now I was going to have a lot less time. We came to the conclusion that the only way forward now was to sell the shop and we put that into motion.

I had an office in Northampton which was where the supervisor also controlled the shops. He was more responsible for the sales etc. and keeping the budget up and that, and the debt was only a secondary thing for him. He was very good to me, he just let me get on with the job, all I had to do was to keep him informed as to where I was going. Whether I was doing a good job or not would certainly show in the figures in two or three months' time. Fortunately I was a success, and it showed in the debt percentage of the region over some three months or so that what we were doing was in fact helping with the total debt control. I was able to give some help in our greengrocery shop – there were days when I would leave around lunchtime and others I would be working there through the evening and therefore I was able to do something. But now the main person was Mummie, and as always she was very confident, people liked her and she got a great deal of help from customers who knew the whole position.

Our social life was somewhat disturbed but when I was in Oxford I used to stay overnight at the Mitre hotel and on many a Saturday night Peggy and I would have an evening meal there and then stay at the hotel overnight and come back the next day. That was when my expenses sheet was very handy. We also used to go to a restaurant in St. Albans on a Saturday to have a meal and as we drove back, we often pulled into a layby and made love to each other there and then. I might tell you that when we got home we simply carried on together in that way. There was nothing that we wouldn't do for each other; we both lived for each other and continued on that way for the rest of our lives.

Martin now had two children, Melissa and Warren, and Jackie was becoming an item with John Fellowes who lived in St. Albans. Lesley had her son who she named Matthew. Roland was teaching at Faraday School and Roz, his wife, was a primary school teacher, however she very quickly gained a promotion and for many years she was a headmistress. John Fellowes used to come to Hobbs Hill Road regularly and more often than not I took him back to St. Albans. We liked John very much and he was obviously happy and Jackie was happy that they were together.

Life went along fairly smoothly. Mummie was very busy and she had her mother to look after and was also still giving piano lessons to pupils and working in the shop. What a girl Mummie was. Make no mistake, we were all very lucky to be with such a very special person. Harold Culpin and I were getting on well. He told me that the head clerks all loved that lovely John Skelton. I was quite flattered although I had to admit that I held their hands and pointed them in the right direction, I didn't take the bull at the gate method.

We are now getting to the end of 1972, when Martin came to tell us that he was thinking of emigrating to Australia. It was a big blow to us, because in those days when you went to Australia or New Zealand you would say goodbye to your family and the likelihood was that you were never going to see each other again. He thought his children would have a better lifestyle than in the UK. Obviously we could say nothing other than good luck, with a very heavy burden in our hearts.

12

In early 1973 I was called to a meeting with Tom Bentley the finance director and the personnel director. First there were congratulations on my success and what I'd done, and then they went straight in and said, 'We want you to move to Glasgow.' Tom outlined the proposition; I was to be the deputy credit manager with the power to change things, of course a manager would have to be involved as well. It was the credit office for Scotland where decisions had to be taken as to whether we could give someone the OK for their proposed hire purchase agreement. Computerisation was now taking over slowly and we relied heavily on information contained in our computer bank, but it was still a personal position and the acceptability of a particular hire purchase amount was still down to a personal decision.

The proposal to me was that they would double my salary, put me in the pension scheme from when I first started as a part time collector and I would go into the scheme without making any contributions at all. The proviso was that I had to make up my mind at that precise moment and be prepared to go to Scotland that night. However it was also part of the deal that if I did not like the job in three months I could return to my old job but would then revert to the conditions that I was now working under. When I explained my situation at home I was told not to worry, the company would transport and look after the whole of my family for three days – that was the time they imagined it would take us to complete the move. I had to ring Mummie and what did she say? Just as I'd expected, 'You always know what to do John, you will only do what is best for us all.'

I returned from Scotland on the Thursday; of course there were lots of questions to be asked. There were really very few answers, my mind was in a whirl and what did the future hold for us? Only time would tell. I had no idea exactly what was really happening, all I knew was that we were moving from Hemel Hempstead, where we had lived for a great many years, and travelling four hundred miles north to somewhere we had never been before.

It meant that I used to fly up to Scotland on the Monday morning and return on the Friday afternoon directly after lunch. I did not need the car in Scotland as I was staying in a nice hotel, very close to my office. First there was the introduction of me to the staff and then after some time the difficult task of changing a few things. It was an Englishman going to Scotland to tell

Scottish people how they should be doing certain things that they were not doing so far. I found out very quickly that whenever you ask the question, 'Why do you do something this way?' inevitably the answer will always be, 'Because we have always done it this way.' The staff appeared to like me and I got along very well with the manager, Norrie Beatty.

Peggy came on a couple of visits and liked Glasgow and so the decision to stay was made. It meant that I had soon found East Kilbride, which was about eight miles from Glasgow. Strangely enough the architect of the new town in East Kilbride was the same man who was the architect of the new town of Hemel Hempstead, and he did it with making separate areas, having a town centre and then different areas coming off that town centre just like in Hemel Hempstead. As I knew in my mind that I was going to accept the job, I had to start looking for rented accommodation. There was the system of the transfer from one council rented property to another and I found a couple of people in East Kilbride in a very nice area, a four bedroomed house which was in an area classed as managerial housing. The people who were in the house wanted to get back south as they were retiring and Hemel Hempstead seemed to fit into their plans.

In the meantime of course things were happening at home; I had been away for some two months. Jackie at seventeen was getting engaged to John Fellowes; Lesley had made some connection with John Jackman who lived in Hobbs Hill Road. The sale of the shop was going ahead and the chances of it being sold seemed possible so that the move to Scotland and the sale of the lease would fit in very nicely. I told Tom Bentley that I'd accept the job and so the time for me to go was set sometime in the middle of August. The move would take some three days, Pickfords would come in, pack up all our belongings while the family went by taxi to be housed in a hotel close to Heathrow airport. The contents of the house would be coming on the second day while Lesley and Matthew, Peggy's mother, Jackie and I travelled by plane to Glasgow, staying at another hotel in East Kilbride for the second night. All of these expenses were paid for by the company, I do not know the total cost but it would have been considerable.

The van arrived on the third day, when unpacking started. It was only Mummie and I who went to the house, the others stayed at the hotel for their meals. We did have a little struggle with the men who tried not to unpack, but I was adamant because I knew that the company had paid for that to happen. They didn't like that too much but in the end they realised just what they had to do. The weather when we arrived was very good indeed and the neighbours were absolutely excellent, about as brilliant as you could possibly imagine.

How we found how very nice our neighbours were was that in the first few days I was talking over the fence to the guy next door who was the manager of a wholesale meat company. He asked how we were getting on and I pulled his leg really, by telling him, 'It was all OK but I'm a bit short of money after all the expenses that we've had.' Do you know, that night, through the door came an envelope and in it was a £10 note! Now remember we are talking about 1973. I'd known this guy perhaps three or four days and he put this money in an envelope with a note saying, 'Pay me back when things get a little better'. I was embarrassed but I had to go back to him and tell him. He was very nice and he said, 'Well I just thought it was neighbourly, to help out somebody who was arriving in Scotland for the first time.' That is how those neighbours in Ballochmyle were. It was a cul-de-sac and we were just a little group of people who enjoyed meeting each other. Peggy looked after both her mother and Matthew when Lesley was at work. I used to take Matthew swimming along with two or three of his friends. We used to go to the cafeteria after the swim when Matthew told his friends to order what they liked because his grandad was a millionaire!

I was in Scotland for some four years and every weekend, weather permitting, Peggy and I travelled extensively. North, south, east, west, Isle of Arran, Isle of Skye, we sat in the Kirk which is a church that the Queen used in Balmoral, and we went to the Cairngorms, not skiing of course but to look at the scenery. Loch Lomond was one of our favourite places but we visited many towns and cities, and when I used to go to work on Mondays the girls were obviously keen to know where we had been that weekend. We travelled a few thousand miles through Scotland. What will follow now is a piece that Peggy wrote for the magazine that we used to have monthly in Elizabeth House and it talks about our visit to Scotland.

"On Loch Lomond there is a boat named The Maid of the Loch and it's a boat that takes people sight-seeing around the whole of the loch, except that on a Wednesday night what happens is it is party night and people from Glasgow come down by train, the train goes right beside the loch and they bring their drinks etc., and there's a band that plays and there's a whole load of people singing and dancing and Martins' Ann loved that trip. In fact when she was in Scotland the last thing that she would have wanted to miss would have been the trip on a Wednesday night to this party. Well, all I can tell you without fear of contradiction is that it just shows how Scottish people know how to party. Ann absolutely loved it. Another thing that she liked was to visit Sauchiehall Street on the Saturday night and watch those people who were fuelled with alcohol and the antics that they got up to while in this state of drunkenness. They were past redemption but Ann loved it and there again she would not have come to Glasgow without visiting Sauchiehall Street on a Saturday night."

Joan Ed.

A SASSENACHS VIEW OF HOGMANAY

In 1973 John was transferred by his Company to Scotland, so the whole family living at home at the time, moved to begin a new life in East Kilbride near Glasgow.

In those days, Christmas was not celebrated very much, there were few Christmas trees or coloured lights in windows, but when we returned to London in 1977, things were changing. Many more houses had Christmas trees and Christmas was entering more into the festivities. In fact the first year we were there, John had to go into work at the Office on both Christmas Day and Boxing Day which was a bit of a culture shock. All their festivities were designed around the New Year, although lots of factories closed for two whole weeks.

For days beforehand the housewives were cleaning and washing and polishing their houses from top to bottom, changing curtains and scurrying about in readiness for a clean new start to the New Year. The old tradition is that fires were laid but not lit before Midnight, to keep the range clean for the New Year. In our area this was not necessary as we all had under floor heated properties.

My first inkling of something different afoot, was when I went to the library on New Years Eve, for books to keep my Mother happy over the holiday period. The library closed at mid-day and the roads leading to the centre had an entirely different feel about them. Cars were flying everywhere all over the road, the atmosphere was electrifying and the Square just before mid-day was full of lurching bodies, the celebrations were already underway. On reaching the library, I was amazed to find several drunken men inside, the quiet peace of the library and the No Speaking signs quite forgotten. I arrived home hot foot, before I was flattened by a speeding, weaving motorist. The excitement in the air was something we had not experienced before or since we left.

My neighbours had warned me that if we did not want callers on New Year's Night, you must have all the lights out in your house, back and front, before midnight. If you left your lights on you were then signalling that you were willing for anyone, stranger or friend to come into your house and partake of your hospitality. All those prepared to entertain had been working like beavers in their kitchens for many hours.

Everything went very quiet to the run up to Midnight, but at 12 o'clock World War Three broke out.

As we were new to the area and the ritual, our neighbours came to us
first to take us on the rounds. The man with the darkest hair always
enters the house first with a piece of coal. The expected thing to

do is to take a plateful of goodies and a drink with you, also a small
present for the lady of the house and to put it under a cushion, or on
a shelf, for her to find when cleaning the room later. My immediate
neighbour used to make some lovely small Scottish Pancakes made on a
Griddle and smothered in butter, also a fudge slab made with condensed
milk and known locally as TABLET, and some Coconut Ice. So Gina would
go with these cut up in portions, on a plate. Someone else did a nice
line in egg and onion sandwiches, very tasty. Another would make a
Clutie, (or Cloutie) Dumpling which is made with suet and lots of fruit
spices etc, made into a large round shape and wrapped in a linen cloth
and boiled in a saucepan. This very often took the place of Christmas
Pudding, I believe, and was always spoken of in very reverent terms.
This could be eaten hot or cold, and was very nice with butter spread
on it. Another person would have a large pot of Scottish Soup on the
go, I believe I put the recipe in the Magazine some time ago.

Anyway, on this particular year we all went off to Norma's house because
she was well known for her parties. By this time, we were all getting
a bit full up with goodies and assorted drinks, so everyone sat around
in a large circle, and was supposed to do a 'turn'. This was always a
bit of a problem for me, as there was not often a piano around, and having
a voice like a Tom Cat, and good ear for music, and not being too hot on
joke or story telling, John would often have to do a double spot for me !
Then after lots of fun and laughter everyone would go on to another house,
and get a steaming bowl of soup and veg. I soon found out why the food
shops were full of packs of three loaf sized cakes, one of Madeira,
one of Sultana and one of Cherries. These were cut into chunks and
handed round in most houses.

Having an old lady at home and a young baby, we could not stay out all
night, but people were still going in and out of houses when we got up
in the morning. One household opposite was still going 36 hours later.

We had always wondered why Scotland took two weeks holiday at Christmas
and New Year, but soon discovered that one week was for preparation,
several days of celebration and the rest of the time for recovery.

Every New Years Night, we think with affection of our friends and neighbours
in Scotland, and our big welcome into the Hogmanay Festivities.

Peggy (with aides from John),   211.

Sadly, before we went to Glasgow, Jackie and John broke off their engagement. There was no alternative for them really – Jackie being only seventeen did have to come with us, and John was at that time starting in his career and also lived with his mother and so the engagement was broken off.

The next thing that happened to us was that Martin and Ann returned from Australia, they were only out there for some eight months. Apparently Ann became desperately home sick and nothing would convince her that their life was to be better in Australia. What she said was that she knew as she went up the steps of the aircraft to fly out that she was making a mistake, and she should never have gone, and from that moment onwards she simply did not settle. She didn't like the place, she didn't like the environment, she didn't like some of the horrible spiders and so they came back. They had to find accommodation and Martin had to find a job and I'm pleased to say that, on both those counts, he was successful. In fact as far as his employment was concerned he never looked back from that moment.

Then we had the very sad news that Roland and Roz were going to break up. I had a letter from Roland dated, I think, 2 December 1974, a very sad letter indeed and quite private. He said that both he and Roz had had quite a difficult time over the last two years and that they had decided they would spend Christmas apart. He wanted to know whether he was still welcome to come to us in Ballochmyle. Of course he was and I replied in that sort of manner. The sad part of the story was that they had a baby, born in the August, named Sophie and he was actually leaving his wife and his four-month-old child to break up the marriage. The family was totally stunned we simply could not believe this was happening. We could not understand how somebody with the character and the temperament of Roland, who was quite a soft sort of personality, could do such a thing.

What came out eventually was that at Roland's school there was a young teacher named Shirley Marshall, who had just lost her husband, and Roland apparently befriended her and the association became quite close. Shirley herself decided that she would quit the country, she was a sports teacher and she got herself a job in a private school in Nassau in the Bahamas, so there was a breakaway point there but not for very long. Roland did come to us for Christmas and I can tell you it wasn't the happiest Christmas of our lives. It was not long before he also got a job at the same school as Shirley Marshall and went out there and of course they lived together in the Bahamas.

We were in touch with Roz and Sophie on numerous occasions and they were regular visitors to Scotland. It wasn't just a question of a duty to us, we liked Roz very much, as I've said previously she was more of a daughter than a daughter-in-law.

Jackie was always a little unhappy with living in Scotland as you can well imagine, after breaking off her engagement. She did get employment and she did have her nights out with her friends and she did meet up with a very nice girl friend and they were real buddies together. When Jackie was eighteen she decided that she would like to go back to England and there was no reason why she should not, and so she and her friend decided to apply to Butlins and work in a holiday camp. I think the first one was at Clacton, I'm not sure about that but it certainly was Butlins, where she would have accommodation. She would go down there with her friend and see what was in store for her back in England. We parted on very good terms, we told her that she was always welcome to come back whenever she wanted to. There was no real argument about it, she was always a person who knew exactly what she wanted and how she was able to obtain it. What happened is that she met up with John again and they got together. Both Jackie and John were also regular visitors to Scotland and came and saw us in Ballochmyle many times, which we were very pleased about. To us, all that mattered was that she was quite happy and settled.

We had an unfortunate car accident in Scotland. It was at a time when Martin and Ann and the children and both Ann's mother and step-father were there as well. We were all going to Ayr, to the coast, for a day's outing and we were going along the motorway very steadily, in two cars of course as there were quite a number of us. A car on the other side of the road started to overtake and he clipped the back wing of the car he was trying to overtake, which threw him onto our side of the road. There was an almighty crash and the car that I was driving was turned upside down and almost into a ditch. Fortunately there were no very serious injuries although for a time it looked nasty because we were tipped upside down and trying to get out. The other car ended up in the ditch – the driver himself was in the ditch with his car, and it turned out that he was drunk. When the police arrived he was drinking out of his half bottle of scotch. The long and short of it all was that this chap was charged. He pleaded not guilty – that the business of him drinking after he'd had the accident was the reason why he was over the limit; he wasn't over the limit at the time of the accident etc. There was to be a court case, and people were coming up from London. Ann and one or two others were coming as witnesses, but at the last minute he pleaded guilty and therefore there was no need for anybody to attend the court. You know to this day I forget just what his sentence was but I guess it doesn't really matter, we all got out of it OK in the end. It was pretty horrendous at the time because the car behind us didn't know what was happening, we were upside down and it was an absolute mess. It was one of those things that you never quite forget.

On a happier note, John Jackman followed Lesley to Scotland after a month or two and eventually they decided to get married. So there was a wedding on 19 March 1976, a quiet wedding but an enjoyable reception at Ballochmyle.

During the last couple of years in Scotland I was asked if I would become a member of what in Scotland is called the 'Children's Panel'. In England it would be called the Juvenile Court; three people would sit in judgement on juveniles, very young offenders. I accepted the opportunity and I did the training. It was quite an experience and gave you an insight into how young offenders can be badly treated by their parents and how the whole family break-up takes place and children go awry. We could do the normal sentencing which in court went right up to sending them to a special school, which in London in those days we would call a borstal, down to them just doing a community service or similar. I can't say I enjoyed that experience. I can't enjoy seeing these sorts of things and it seemed to be happening all the time, because of the number of cases that you dealt with. But it was interesting and it gave me an insight into how the behaviour of some families is so out of step with what one would call normal living.

I think we had been in Scotland a couple of years, and we were in constant contact of course with Roland, when he sent us some money as the air fare from Scotland to Nassau, in the Bahamas. I'm not sure now whether it was for a birthday or anniversary but it was something like that and arrangements were made for a holiday, I think we went for two or three weeks but I wouldn't be absolutely sure. Of course we were going to meet Shirley Marshall for the first time. We were still a bit unhappy but there was nothing that we could do about the situation, it was his choice and we felt that we simply had to go and meet this young lady with whom he was now obviously in partnership. We had a good time in the Bahamas and Shirley treated us very well. The school that they were at was a private school, where the teaching staff were mostly English and the headmaster himself was English. It appeared that Bahamian mothers and fathers liked their children to go to this particular private school. I used to take Roland and Shirley to school and then use his car during the day to travel around the island and the beautiful beaches there. At weekends quite a few of the teachers, who all had their own boats, would go to the famous island and dive over the side to pick up crawfish off the floor of the sea. Then we would be taken ashore and a barbecue would be built and we would have these very fresh crawfish and salad. There was nothing much else to do there other than to swim, sit in the sunshine and enjoy the weather. We did go to the casino once or twice. Residents were not allowed to bet themselves, but of course Roland would pass me some money beforehand and then I was able to place his bets for him. So everything really went according to plan and we did have a very nice time there.

One particular incident which we always remember is that the flat Roland and Shirley were in was owned by a builder who was quite friendly with Roland and who was, well, a millionaire I would think many times over. Anyway at the time he bought himself a new boat, a really very nice boat indeed. He decided that he would like to take Roland's mum and dad out for a trip for the weekend, with Roland and Shirley, and that was arranged. The only problem was that when we did get out we had some very rough seas – but just before then we were doing some fishing off the back of the boat and I caught a magnificent fish. They said that it was a small dolphin. I'm not sure that it was, but it was a big fish and I do have a photograph. We took it aboard and we killed it, hit it in the head with a mallet, cooked it and ate it. Unfortunately the weather turned very bad, very rough indeed and so we had to call in to another little island where this builder had a friend who owned the island. He lived on it almost alone, although he did have a rather nice young lady there who he was obviously living with and one of his jobs was to sell plots of land off this island to rich people.

What a catch!

The weather turned really bad and we had to stay the night with him in this house. Roland and Shirley had to get to school the next day and so the builder, who had a plane and a pilot, phoned his pilot to come over and pick Roland and Shirley up first and then come back for Mummie and me. I can tell you

Life in the Bahamas

Shirley holding live lobster!

that was not a journey I would like to do again because it was just a very small plane. When it ran along the runway it was bumping all over the place because the runway on that little island was not flat and it was, well, I suppose you could say terrifying. But it did take off and it did land safely but that's about as much as I could say. Our hearts were in our mouths all the time. It was another one of those experiences that you don't forget very quickly.

I should have known that there was something afoot when Peggy told me that at a function with Tom Bentley, a dinner and dance of some description, Tom had danced with Peggy and spoke to her as though she was a friend. Apparently he had said to her, 'John is an extremely valuable asset to the company,' but explained it did mean in those circumstances that from time to time John had to move. Well we had realised that by virtue of the fact of coming to Glasgow, but I had no idea what my next move was going to be. I quickly found out because I was called to Nottingham and once again met Tom Bentley and the Personnel Director who said to me that they wanted me to come back to England and to split up the credit office, which was a large office in Houndsditch, in London. It had become too cumbersome and they wanted to split it in half – it would be my job to start an office right from the beginning. A space would be made available at the back of a Cavendish store in Finchley. The rest of it had not been dealt with and I would be going down there, on my own without any interference, to set up this office and deal with the builders and decorators. New staff would have to be taken on, and they would have to be trained. It was hoped the whole thing could be up and running in around about three months. I was told that I would have no interference from anybody, I would be totally responsible for doing this job and all that was necessary was for me to keep Tom Bentley informed as to the progress.

I was asked if I thought I was up to the job and I said, 'Well, of course I am.' Once again the business of confidence without a great deal of ability came to the fore. It was a great opportunity for me to break into what would be senior management. Then there was the question of housing. I was told not to worry about that because the company owned quite a lot of property and there was a house that they had found that would be quite suitable for me in Crouch End. It was a five bedroomed, three storey place attached to a Cavendish furniture shop. That was a very, very big apartment. I would go down there and the deal would be that I would live there rent and rates free and would not have to pay anything for my electricity etc. I would have a fairly large increase in salary. I would have a company car and normal expenses etc. I couldn't believe what I was being offered. I accepted and they said, 'Well from today onwards you will not be attached to the office in

Glasgow.' Although I had to wait to go and live in the accommodation, I would be expected to go to Crouch End and stay in a hotel, and the office was to be in North Finchley.

I was really shaking. I had to go back and tell Mummie what was going to happen and that we were once again on the move. Unfortunately by this time her mother was very frail. She didn't want to go back and she was going to go into a home, but then she died just previous to Peggy actually moving from Scotland to Crouch End. It was some three or four months before Peggy actually came down to Crouch End. The same procedure took place, I went down on Monday mornings and came back Friday afternoon for a month or two. I changed it slightly after then but I'll tell you about that when the time comes. I have to say that during this period Lesley was very helpful to Mummie in looking after nannie and took some of the stress from Mummie. Well done Lesley.

I stayed in a hotel in Muswell Hill and quickly went to see the house in Crouch End, a nice house, but in need of almost total redecoration. I informed Tom about this and he said not to worry, all I had to do was to tell them what decoration was required, the curtains that should go up, the wallpaper and the carpets and it would all be done before the family moved down. I got in touch with Roz because she was the type of person who was into interior decorating. She came to Crouch End and looked around and she bought catalogues and all sorts of things. She chose the curtains and wrote their numbers down, she chose the wallpaper etc. All this was sent to Nottingham and there was no argument, they agreed to do everything that was on the list. I cannot tell you what the cost was but it would not have been cheap at all. They obviously wanted me back doing this particular job.

I then had to start what was actually going to be done in the North Finchley office. There was just a fairly large room, so I had to deal with the builders, well not exactly builders, they were decorators but they were people the company always dealt with. They came and I told them what was necessary and they obviously put their price in and that was all there was to that. They needed to put a partition up so I had an office of my own but other than that it was pretty straightforward. Dealing with the computer people was not quite as straightforward because we were in the early stage of computerisation and I knew very little about computers, and that's the way it stayed for the rest of my life, but I had to pretend that I did know just a little bit. If I am honest, I was lost in that department but I somehow or another got through the problem. Then the most difficult part was the question of staff. I went to the meetings at the labour exchange to see what the potential was. I told them what the situation was, that over the course of the next two or three months I would want some twelve to fourteen people. I would be taking on maybe in the first instance a couple of people, then maybe two or four, I didn't know. They thought it would not be too much of a problem and in actual fact it turned out that they were quite right.

I had many decisions to make but it never became too much of a problem to me because I was the sort of person who felt that once a decision had been made it was no longer a problem. Tom Bentley was quite fair and quite right that there was no question of interference whatsoever from Nottingham, once I'd made a decision it was only a question of me telling them, as opposed to saying, 'Is this OK?' They held to their word that they would leave the whole project to me. I felt quite honoured really but meanwhile I thought to myself many times, 'This is a boy who left school at thirteen and a half without a single qualification and I am now telling lots of people what to do.'

By this time the computers and the telephone system were in and the office furniture that we required was arriving. So I decided I would start to interview people to see who was actually available on the market. I engaged two young ladies, they came from India, very intelligent and about thirty or thirty-five years old, both married and very keen to learn the part that they were going to have to play in the office. I kept an eye on the decoration of the house in Crouch End and it appeared to me that it would not be too long before we would be moving down from Scotland. I then engaged a further two people, after the original two had been working for a couple of weeks. One of these people came from Zimbabwe and the other was an English girl and they both settled in very well. At that time we were only working on what we call dummy papers. I informed Nottingham that I thought we were ready to receive papers from perhaps four or six shops. The house in Crouch End was completed, the decoration was done, it looked very good indeed and so I then had to start making the move back to London.

Lesley and John Jackman had their own flat with Matthew, Jackie was back in the south, and Peggy's mother had died. So in this last house it was just Mummie and me. I guess it was the first time for ages that we were on our own. The move went OK and we actually found when we arrived that we were living next door to Annie Lennox and Dave Stewart. What a surprise and what very nice people they were, and I'll tell you a little more later about our association with them in the time that we actually lived in Crouch End.

Before we left Scotland, when we heard Roz and Roland's marriage was breaking down, I wrote to my mother and told her about it. I'm afraid that she didn't take it too kindly and I guess that she thought back to the time that she was left with four children. However, she sent rather a nasty letter to Roland telling him that he was no longer welcome in her house, and so I'm afraid I had to write to her and tell her that as long as she felt like that I would have to take it that neither Mummie nor I would be welcome, and so there was a breakaway from the family. For many years I was not in contact with either her or any of my brothers and sister over that particular instance. When she died many years later Roland did go to her funeral because he realised that I would feel better if he did attend and pay his last respects.

When we were packing up to come down to Crouch End, we had to decide what to do with all the letters Mummie wrote to me every day while I was away during the war. I kept them all and she also kept her letters, which meant that we had boxes and boxes of letters. We decided that we would destroy them, on the basis – and I agreed with this at the time – that we were getting much older and all that would happen would be that the children and other people to get hold of them and most probably laugh about them. They were our love letters, and we destroyed them. It was a mistake, a very serious mistake which we realised many years later because they would have meant a great deal to us in our later life if we could just read them over. However the mistake was made, they were destroyed and we didn't keep one of them. Why we didn't keep one I really don't know, and I've never understood why we both felt at that time that they should all be destroyed.

The other story about Scotland is that the family once decided to have a caravan holiday in Skegness. John and Lesley and Matthew came, Martin and Ann came with Melissa and Warren, and Jackie and John also came so it was a real family holiday. I took the children down onto the beach one day, with their usual packed lunches, sandwiches etc, wind breaks and all that sort of equipment for the children. I was always happy to be with the children but Warren decided that what he would do is kick sand over the sandwiches. I tried to stop him on two or three occasions but it was of no use. So I went to him and gave him one hearty smack across the calf of his leg. Unfortunately for me, just at that very moment Ann appeared on the scene. All I can tell you is that world war three started. It's a story which has been told many times during our get togethers and no doubt it will never be forgotten.

Just before we were moved from Scotland, during the period that I was actually in Crouch End on my own and Mummie was living in Scotland, Jackie and John had got engaged. They fixed their wedding for 5 February 1977 and of course it meant lots of arrangements etc. We were very pleased for them; we went down to the wedding, which was in St. Albans. On the day Jackie looked stunning, she was a very nice looking girl and on her wedding day she looked absolutely beautiful. I was extremely proud when I walked her up the aisle. I knew that she and John were really happy together and I was glad that our four children were now married.

As I have said, there was just the two of us now to come down. The furniture was packed up in the normal way and I was going to bring my car down on the night train service, which meant I drove it to Waverly station in Edinburgh, we went to the theatre that night and then I think we boarded the train at around ten o'clock or so. We were in a sleeper and were travelling first class, I was now in senior management and so I was able to upgrade. It was a very comfortable journey and we had a nice breakfast when we'd arrived and then drove over to Crouch End, as I've said, to find that we were living next door to Annie Lennox and Dave Stewart.

We got on very well with them, very well indeed. They were not called the Eurhythmics then, they were called the Tourists and they had very little money. They thought that we were quite rich, particularly after we bought our caravan in Hayling Island, which we did to give ourselves a weekend retreat. I can tell you that they were in poor straits at that time, to say the least, their living conditions were not as one might expect. Peggy and Annie got on very well because they were both students of the Royal Academy of Music. Peggy didn't actually attend the Royal Academy but was taught by a teacher of the Royal Academy, whereas Annie actually went to the Royal Academy and studied as a flautist, that's quite surprising but that's what she studied at the Royal Academy. Annie dropped out because she wanted to take the path of being something quite different from a flautist in a band. They got on very well did Annie and Mummie, and Dave as well, he used to chat away. They had an old van which they used to tour in. I remember a time when they were going to Germany to tour and they couldn't get it started, I had to give them a push. They were going to sleep in the van, they weren't going to stay in hotels. We met Annie's mother and father very regularly because they were quite concerned about them, the way they were living or whether they were ever going to make it. Obviously they were a little bit upset from time to time when they saw the conditions that they were living in, but as we all know it all turned out well for them in the end. I can tell you that the first song that Annie Lennox wrote she called 'Flowers' after looking over from her patio onto our patio where we always had a very good display of hanging baskets full of colourful flowers.

Roland and Shirley came back from the Bahamas to get married. Their wedding took place on 31 December 1979 and it was held at Shirley's parents' house which was in Scunthorpe. We were all going and we went in convoys in separate cars. Along the way when we were pretty close to their house we pulled into a layby and we changed into the dress that one would expect people to wear coming from the Bahamas – grass skirts, made-up faces and all the paraphernalia of the Bahamian as opposed to English people. We arrived at Shirley's mother and fathers' house and I can tell you that we were not well received by Shirley's mother. Her father followed in to the celebrations but her mother was certainly not going to be part of it. We moved quickly on to Shirley's sister, Jackie, and there we had some real good laughter and entertainment. Jackie and her husband and their children were all part and parcel of the Bahamian contingent that came for the wedding. Shirley's father was a tremendous DIY man, he could do anything with his hands and he had covered the bar in their house with some leather padding. Unfortunately during the party somebody must have spilt cigar ash on it and burnt a hole. It meant that for the rest of the time one of the party had to either be standing with their elbow over it or it had to be covered up so that it wasn't noticed by Shirley's father. However the wedding went off OK and Shirley and Roland were now Mr and Mrs Skelton.

Mummie at this time was on her own during the day and she felt that what she would like to do was to get some employment to keep her mind active. I thought it was a very good idea. She managed to get a job which was only one hundred yards or so from where we lived, with a small company called John Dron. It was a mail order company where there were about ten employees and she would be the comptometer operator. She enjoyed it. I can't remember whether she was full time or not, I think in actual fact she was pretty much full time but I don't really remember the exact hours. There she met a young lady named Mary McKenna, who was a lady who had been divorced and had two teenaged sons. Unfortunately for Mary she had a mental problem, not so severe that she couldn't work but she was certainly one of those people who are full of anxieties and troubles etc. Mummie being Mummie, she took her under her wing and decided that she would look after Mary. She made a real friend of Mary and stuck up for her in the office from time to time, so much so that Mary and her two sons used to come to our caravan. We also invited them one Christmas dinner I remember, and they struck up a very strong friendship, we knew all about Mary and her family and she knew all about our family. When we left Crouch End they stayed friends for the rest of Mummie's life, mostly through letters but they were regular letter writers to each other, very newsy, always about the family etc. Unfortunately I think for Mary one son was a Tottenham supporter and the other son was an Arsenal supporter – I don't think I need to say more than that but they were on opposite sides of the fence.

Sophie and Roz were regular visitors on numerous weekends. They came to the caravan in Hayling Island – there was never a question of could they come or not, there were other people who did come, but generally speaking I would say Sophie and Roz were the most regular. Martin, Ann, Melissa and

116

Warren came and I can tell you a little story. Our caravan was actually in the back garden of a bungalow but there was a caravan park called Elliott's caravan park nearby and on Saturday nights they used to have regular Saturday entertainment. We used to go over there quite regularly, and one Saturday when Martin, Ann, Melissa and Warren were there, we went over and there was a competition. It was for young children, I can't remember the age, to see which child had the loudest voice. Melissa went into this competition, I think there was about twelve other competitors, they were all given the same word to shout. Melissa did her bit and of course it was judged by the audience, by clapping. For the other eleven people there was some mild clapping, for Melissa there was loud clapping and stamping of feet. She was the winner by a mile, a story often told and of course she was quite often named 'the voice' after that shouting exhibition. She has always had a loud voice, as those around her know very well.

My major job at this time was with building up the office and that took up all of my time during the day. We slowly but surely took on one or two more people, we took over some shops and did the credit for those shops and everything was going according to plan. We didn't have any serious problems that weren't overcome from time to time, the girls I took on worked well with each other and I also took on a man named Les Myhill. He was going to be my assistant in the office, all I can say is that it was a very friendly office and within the two or three months that the office was expected to be running, it was running.

Of course living in Crouch End I was able to go and watch Arsenal play on a Saturday afternoon when they were at home, and when Martin and Warren used to come, with their family of course, and stay at Crouch End, they always chose a time when Arsenal would be playing at home. When Warren used to come along we used to take a box with us and he would stand on his box and shout 'Arsenal home'. I think that that's where his affiliation with Arsenal began and it has stayed with him ever since. Ann also became a great Arsenal fan and I think it all started from those days in Crouch End. You'll remember from the beginning of the book that I watched Arsenal in 1938 so I had been an Arsenal supporter for many years.

We had some very good Christmases in Crouch End, the family came and like all of our family Christmases or get togethers, they are always very competitive. The games and so on were very well organised, the television would go off on Christmas eve and it certainly didn't come on again until well after Boxing day. We were good organisers with Christmas parties right down to the fact that we would have a list of jobs that had to be done and who was doing them at any particular time so you always knew whether you were free of some washing up or wiping up, or whether you were actually the washer up yourself. I'm afraid there was an unfortunate incident when Martin had a dog called Rinty, which was also the name of our dog in Hobbs Hill Road. The front door was left open, well we only had one door really at Crouch End, and the dog ran off. Unfortunately we never saw that dog again.

While we were there we had a holiday, it was a coach and camping holiday in France, the name of the place as far as I can remember was Hyeres. Sophie and Roz came, Jackie and John came and Peggy and myself and we went on this camping holiday. It was a very long journey, we got tired but we were able to travel from there to San Tropez, we went to Monte Carlo and we went to the Palace de Marco where Prince Rainier and Grace Kelly lived, we had a very nice time. Unfortunately, while we were there, there was a wind which apparently is known as the Mistral and that blew for several days but never the less we all had a very good time. It was a tiring journey back, not the sort of journey that you would want to take too often but never the less we all had a good time travelling around. We were on the beach of course but we enjoyed seeing places that we hadn't seen before.

We used to walk over Hampstead Heath, a great many times, we knew Hampstead Heath like the back of our hands. Also we used to go to London and walk around the city and we got to know London extremely well; we could really have been London guides towards the end. The places that we went to were HMS *Belfast* and the house of horrors, along Whitehall through Horse Guards Parade and then through the park to the Palace and back along the Mall to Trafalgar Square and then up to St. Paul's. We did a lot of walking and we found both Hampstead Heath and London itself was the sort of place that you could go to over and over again and see something different each time.

Roland and Shirley came back for a period and came to Crouch End, I'm not sure what the occasion was, whether it was some special occasion or not, that's gone past my memory. What I do know and remember is that Shirley's mother and father and her sister Jackie and her husband and their children all came to Crouch End for that particular weekend. We went and met them at Heathrow and then we came back and had quite a big party. I can't remember who came from our family but there were certainly a lot of members of our family there. We took the opportunity to walk Shirley's mother and father and her sister around London and showed them a few of the London sites. I do know that they thoroughly enjoyed it because Shirley's sister Jackie and the children often spoke about the time that they came to visit Crouch End.

13

I had been in Crouch End, I would think for some three years, and the office was going well. We had settled into a routine of going to the caravan at the weekends and then we had our normal sorts of holidays, we certainly went to many parts of Spain, Benidorm and further down were our tourist places. We also went to Italy, Malta, and Rome and of course we spent quite a few weekends in Paris because we simply loved walking around Paris.

But then I was called to Nottingham to meet Tom Bentley, he hadn't given me any idea of what it was about. He said that the office was running very well and congratulated me on the way it had been set up. I was quite pleased about that, but the manager in London was going to retire and Tom wanted me to run the London office and at the same time be responsible for North Finchley. Les Myhill who was my assistant in North Finchley would generally run the show while I would be responsible for it and that I would then be responsible for taking over from the manager in Houndsditch, where the office was. It meant that instead of just the forty shops I was now to be responsible for eighty or so shops.

Of course it was a big surprise, but an even bigger one was that unfortunately I had to get out of Crouch End because that property was going to be sold. They had found another nice three bedroomed apartment in Orpington and that when I left Crouch End I could move there under the same circumstances, rent free etc. But Tom did say, 'Look as far as the decoration is concerned, we know what you like and therefore just leave it to us and we will redecorate the place before you go in.' I guess he was a little sorry that he had to pay so much money the last time that the decoration was done in Crouch End. However I was quite happy with that, although I thought to myself, 'My goodness, now instead of having forty managers of branches phoning me every day I will now have eighty managers.' Although I did hope that some of them would be in touch with Les Myhill in North Finchley. They did, and it turned out that Les himself did quite a good job but I had to travel backwards and forwards from one place to the other on a regular basis to make certain that everything was going according to plan. This was in the early 1980s and we were loaning out a million pounds plus each week and that I was totally responsible for what happened to that money.

Anyway, that was what was going to happen and Tom hoped that it would all be happening within about a month or so. At least I would be in London in a month even if I wasn't back in Orpington because I could travel from Crouch End to London quite easily really. We did move and the apartment was very nice, we had a very nice patio and the rooms were nice, well everything about it was perfectly OK. Mummie was a bit upset that she would have to leave her job with her friend Mary McKenna, but she decided to get another little job and she did a part time job in Greggs the bakers, something quite different for her. She used to work from around about eleven o'clock until three, four or five days a week. She didn't work on Saturday because we were down at the caravan. She enjoyed it, she enjoyed meeting people and talking to people.

So I started in the London office. There was an assistant manager there by the name of Alan Fisher who I had met before. I do remember that he said some of the other managers would ask him, 'What's this guy John Skelton like?' He told me, 'What I tell them is that if you become a friend of his then you're really, really set up because he stands by friends all the time, but if you make yourself an enemy then you have to remember that with John Skelton, you're dealing with dynamite.' I guess that's what did used to happen, that people would quickly find out that I really meant what I said.

We still had the caravan on Hayling Island and I had been in the London office some time and had settled down. We still had our holidays abroad, we still had people come and see us while we were there. Jackie by that time was pregnant and she had her first child Gemma and just shortly before that Shirley had Joanna, who was actually born in the Bahamas, and so there were another two grandchildren. Gemma was born on the fourteenth of May, which in fact was Mummie's birthday, and she always said that of all the birthday presents that she'd ever had, this was the best one in the world. A granddaughter born on her birthday. She really meant what she said. We went to see Gemma when she was maybe a day or two old, something like that, and Jackie's first words to us were, 'You won't like her, you won't like her mum.' Mummie said, 'Why's that?' and Jackie said, 'Well she's got ginger hair.' She did, she had ginger hair which stood up in little spikes. Jackie was quite right that the hair itself was quite strange, it slowly but surely changed colour but we always joked about the ginger-haired baby whose hair stood up in spikes. It's a story which is told over and over and over again.

By this time Roland and Shirley were having to move out of the Bahamas. I can't remember the exact date and time but there was a ruling put through the Bahamian Island that English teachers could only stay in employment in the Bahamas for, I think it was, five years and they had already had eight years. So they had to make arrangements to come back. By this time as I've said Joanna was born and so they came back and they stayed with us in Orpington for around about a year I think it was while Roland and Shirley were settling for what they were going to do. Roland at the time was wondering whether he might open a sports shop, and did all the necessary negotiations but nothing worked out. In the end I got him a job working for me as one of what we used to call the reference men who would call on people – not a debt collector but somebody who was calling on people just to see what their circumstances were like – and he did that for some time. The problem was that I'm afraid Joanna was a little baby who cried constantly, night and day, all the time. She just could not be consoled, no matter what one did. Shirley, her mother, used to cry along with her, it was one of those episodes. Now Joanna herself is a doctor, she's in the Bahamas and it's just another one of those stories – another one of those family stories of the grandchild who cried more often than all the others put together, and that was Joanna. Eventually Martin got Roland a position in Zurich insurance, which Martin worked for and was a senior member of their staff. So what happened was that Roland and Shirley and Joanna moved to Stubbington, which is some two miles outside of Fareham and within a few minutes of Martin and Ann. Their friendship developed and they played golf together and went about together and that is where they have been ever since. They still live, not in the same house of course, but never the less within some few minutes from each other in Stubbington and see each other very regularly. I would say almost on a day to day basis.

Lesley was still in Scotland. She felt, like Mummie and I did, that the Scots were nice people and she liked the place but it was a long way from relatives. People visited of course, they visited us but there was something about living some four hundred miles from nearest relative. She had two more children, Christopher and Simon, brothers to Matthew, but unfortunately she never got the little girl that she always wanted. They came to Hayling Island for holidays in the caravan, but visits were few and far between. I used to travel by car to London, looking the part with my briefcase and umbrella but I never succumbed to wearing a bowler hat, in those days the bosses were always referred to as a mister, I think these days things are a little bit more relaxed.

In January 1984, which was some time before I retired, Lesley and John Jackman came back to England from Scotland. After a very short time, in June '84, they decided to part. That left Lesley on her own as a single mother with three children, a very difficult time for her. She got divorced the next year. Then she met Clive in April 1988 and she did eventually marry him in June 1991.

More grandchildren were on the way. Martin and Ann had Warren, brother to Melissa. Roland and Shirley had Bobby, named after Bobby Charlton, a brother to Joanna. Jackie and John had a brother to Gemma named Jamie. I have to admit now that the ages and birthdays escape my knowledge, you see Mummie dealt with all of those matters when she was alive and so far in my real old age I find attention to that detail quite difficult.

The call that came next was to go to Nottingham. It turned out that we were now having to get out of the London office and the idea was to join the North Finchley office and the London office together. In fact, it would now be in North Finchley and not in London and it was my task to engineer this move, but only three of the London office girls were able to travel to North Finchley so it meant more staff had to be taken on. So I did have an extremely busy time making sure that the changeover was as efficient as it possibly could be. It meant that I had to travel from Orpington to North Finchley and it wasn't an easy journey. It's difficult to remember exactly how long it took but I found in the end it wasn't good for my health and the doctor told me that I now had high blood pressure. I talked to Tom Bentley about it and he told me what I should do is find myself a hotel close to North Finchley and stay there say for three nights a week and the rest of the time go home.

This I did, I found a nice hotel in Enfield, with the nicest food that you could possibly imagine that you could have. It was at a time when I was able to take people there and for them to taste the menu. Roz and Sophie went quite regularly, Jackie and John too, the only person who complained that she never went there was Mummie herself, I don't quite know how that happened but it did. However I was just there for the three nights, I used to stay Tuesday, Wednesday and Thursday nights and the rest of the time I went home.

Although I was away for three nights Mummie and I talked on the telephone every night. This most probably will surprise the children but she was a real tease on the telephone and our conversations quite often were of a sexual sort of nature. I told the children more than once that I was the only person who really knew Mummie.

On Hayling island there was a lot of erosion going on and the authorities started to fill the sandy beach with stone and rubble and bricks and goodness knows what and so the whole atmosphere of the place was totally different. It was no good for us and so we just left the caravan. The man who owned the caravan owned the bungalow where the caravan was; he didn't live there, he let it out as a holiday home. I asked him what I should do, should I tow it away or leave it on site? He said, 'No, just leave it there.'

So that's what we did, we upped and left it, there was no cash changed hands or anything like that, we simply left the caravan and we then had no weekend retreat. It's not to say we didn't go to lots of places during that time, there was hardly a main seaside resort that Mummie and I had not been to.

It was just one of those things. We did like the seaside, we liked the promenades, the piers and those were the sorts of places that we used to like to see. We were regular visitors to the Lake District, we used to go on many occasions, and one of the places that we used to stay at was a bed, breakfast and evening meal in Grange, which is part of the Borrowdale. We also went to the Derbyshire Dales and another one of our favourite places was York. We walked through York Minster many times and enjoyed ourselves just walking through those old cities.

We were extensive travellers really, Mummie loved travelling, she was never bored with travelling in a car as all the children know, the one thing she liked more than anything else was to have a nice journey in the car. Travel to her was one of those things which gave her a great deal of pleasure.

Sophie used to come to my office in North Finchley fairly regularly and the girls knew her. One day she went out into the outer office and said, 'My granddad said ...' I can't quite remember the phrase she used but from that moment onwards I really lost a great deal of authority, and when I went out into the outer office there was always the cry of 'So what does granddad want us to do today?' It was all a joke and it was all taken in that sort of way but it's a story I told at Sophie's wedding when I made my speech and it caused a great deal of laughter – of course, those knowing Sophie would know it would be the sort of thing that she would say.

Even with my hotel stay, the journey was extremely difficult getting to North Finchley and I was really under stress. I was always first in the office and the last to leave and I had to make certain that everything had been catered for during the day. However as I have said before, I never took any problems home. Mummie and I were just as happy with each other as though we had just got married. So I decided to go to Nottingham and see Tom. I told him the position and the pressure that I was under, and asked what could be done about it. His response was that I should find a three bedroom furnished house, which the company would pay for, closer to North Finchley and that is what I did. You'll have to remember that I was not well educated, I was not well read, nor did I ever understand computers to any great extent. What I did know was that the budget for the office which I was in charge of was always on target and the monthly debt percentage was always well below target, and that was really what they were concerned about. I could not say that I was one of those people who were highly paid, I had a reasonable salary with perks which were thrown in and there were many of them which you will appreciate. Mummie and I had a good income and we were saving like mad for our retirement.

Jackie and I started to look for accommodation, possibly in the St. Albans or Hemel Hempstead area. Hemel Hempstead was our favourite because it's close to the M1 and North Finchley is a turning off the M1 and that was really quite an easy journey for me. We did find a three bedroomed house in Hemel and we took on the lease for six months. As usual Mummie just left it to me, which she always did. I've said so many times that she always said, 'John will know what to do.' I would say Jackie most probably organised the thing more than I did but anyway, it all went through. I paid the deposit for the accommodation and the first month's rent I think it was about four hundred and fifty pounds and then the company reimbursed me. The people who were doing the business with us wouldn't deal with the company they only wanted to deal with the person who was actually going to live in the accommodation.

So we left our furniture in Orpington and moved to Hemel Hempstead, we were back where we first started and where we left in 1973, we knew a lot of people, lots of friends and we caught up with them, we were very close to Jackie and John and everything went according to plan. As far as I was concerned the journey backwards and forwards from Hemel to North Finchley was really quite easy in comparison from Orpington to North Finchley, and things started to quieten down. I was not under the same sort of stress as I was previous to the move. However we came to the end of the six months and the people wanted the house back and so I had to find another in Hemel, which I did. We were quite happy with it because we didn't have young children that could muck things up, we were in no way worried about the state of the house. Peggy didn't take on any other employment and she used to meet some of her friends from the old days, so we were quite happy with the way in which the world was treating us.

14

My grandchildren have always loved me telling them what they called 'Granddad stories'. I know that their parents will most probably be saying, 'Oh, he's not going to tell those stories again is he?' But I will put on record two of them that I think are the best ones.

The first is from when Mummie and I were travelling in Africa. We were walking along a river bank and it was crocodile infested. Beside us there was a family with a little boy and the little boy fell into the river. This mighty crocodile was just about to engulf the little boy when I dived in. Fortunately I had with me a rather sharp dagger and I was able to put my arm around the crocodile and stab it in the neck – there was a lot of blood. The blood was spurting from the crocodile, but he was killed and the boy was saved. By that time there were a lot of people on the bank and they were clapping and cheering, saying 'Well done' and 'Well done Granddad', and in that crowd there just so happened to be the Queen and she had with her some medals. She said hello and she said the same sort of thing, 'Well done Granddad. I'll present you with this medal for saving this young child's life, without you he obviously would have been eaten by the crocodile. Well done Granddad.'

Bobby I think was the one who was always interested in this story. I won't tell you the age he was when he heard it last, but it was old enough that you would not suspect it. When I was visiting he would get into my bed and say, 'Tell me the crocodile story Granddad.' He was always interested in questions like: How much blood was there? Where was the blood? How/where was it spurting? Was there a lot of blood? Was the river full of blood?' He was certainly interested in the blood content of the river as opposed to the saving of the child.

My other story is one I'd associate more with Warren, because Warren was always a little boy who loved cars and he particularly loved Rolls-Royces. When I used to go and see him, from time to time, I had a decent company car but it was not the same as a Rolls-Royce. So I used to tell him that in my garage at home there was a Rolls-Royce that did belong to me, but I didn't take it out very often because I didn't want it to get damaged in any way and I only took it on very short distances. Warren was extremely anxious that I should give him a ride in this Rolls-Royce at some time or another, which I promised him I would. Each time I visited he used to ask me about it: 'How's it getting on?' I would tell him, 'Well.'

Until one day he said to me, 'Do you know Granddad, I don't think you have got a Rolls-Royce.' So I immediately said to him, 'Well, Warren. If you don't think that I've got a Rolls-Royce then you'll never have a ride in it. So we'll just leave it at that.'

'Oh well no, no,' he said. 'I didn't mean that you haven't got one. I was just a little bit worried that you might not have one.' His whole tone changed, he was always waiting for that ride in the Rolls-Royce. Of course the ride never came and the Rolls-Royce was never in the garage.

I was also known to be pretty good at getting babies off to sleep when perhaps they were misbehaving and crying. My secret was that you held them tight, right close to yourself and you patted them lightly and slowly on the bottom, while humming 'Go to sleep my baby' softly, gently. They'll soon calm down. With only one exception, it worked every time, and the exception was Joanna.

15

Towards the end of 1986 I was called to Nottingham to be told that GUS had sold the whole of the furniture division to Phil Harris of Carpet Right, and that Phil Harris did not want a credit division because although he did hire purchase it was put out to a finance company called Lombard Trinity. The take-over would take a few months but the whole staff, myself included and others in Nottingham, were actually made redundant. I had to go back and tell them all the details. For an extremely happy office it was difficult to digest. The date set was the end of January 1987. For me it was not such a big blow; I was sixty-two almost sixty-three, I would get my redundancy and my contract was to be paid for six months and that meant I had a very nice nest egg. We knew that we would be able to enjoy our retirement. However there would be the question of housing.

Everyone was extremely upset but they knew that it was not in my hands to alter the decision. Christmas came and went and the girls had been paid up to the end of January but work had by now completely dried up, so I rang to find out what I should do and was told, 'Well, just finish today, we no longer require your office.' That was a blow but there were details to be dealt with. What to do with the petty cash? The answer came back, 'Well, just keep it.' What to do about the furniture? Anything the girls wanted, wardrobes or any desks, they could just have and some of them did hire a van and take a desk and a wardrobe and other bits which were in the kitchen. The computer terminals etc., could be left as they would be dealt with by Phil Harris. I said, 'Do you mean that we should just go home today?' and the answer came back, 'Yes, your office is no longer required, it's all over.' What an ending.

I can tell you that for many years afterwards I had Christmas cards from most of the girls. Mummie always replied, she knew the girls quite well because we did have from time to time office evenings out and Mummie was quite well known to the girls themselves.

We now had to decide what we were going to do about accommodation. I had been supplied with a house for many years and therefore it was now a question of where do we go from here? Peggy and I talked about it but her usual response was 'Well, you'll know what to do John.' I said, 'Why don't I write to the council and see what they've got to offer? We've got this nice sum of money behind us we can go and do just exactly what we want, when

127

we want and how we want.' So I wrote to the council and they wrote back to me to say that yes, as I was homeless, which I would be at the end of March, because of my age and so on they could offer me a flat in Elizabeth House but the place would not be complete until 14 March 1987. We could go and have a look at it and see what the accommodation was like. So we did and we decided that it looked very nice actually. It was a new building and the warden showed us the flat which is of course the one that we are in today.

So the decision was taken that we would keep our money and move into Elizabeth House. What I can tell you is that it was the best or at least one of the best decisions of our lives, we did enjoy every moment that we spent together in Elizabeth House, we were extremely happy. We were able to come and go just when we liked, go where we liked, travel where we liked and we did just that. Of course, we'd got the furniture, which was in Orpington, but a lot of it was too big to bring to Elizabeth House. We organised a sale of this furniture, carpets, curtains and beds etc. In fact we only took to Elizabeth House from Orpington the bureau, which was Mummie's bureau which had belonged to her mother before her, and the bed. We took the furniture by van, Jackie had a nice driveway into her house, and we stacked the furniture up in the driveway and advertised it. I can tell you that within a very short time all of it had gone. We were selling it at knock down prices, all we wanted was to get rid of it, the money side was not important.

While we were still in the rented accommodation, on Fridays I used to look after Jamie. Gemma was at school and so Jamie came to us. I used to take him to the sweet shop which was in Woodhall Farm and he could choose what sort of sweets he'd like and I'd buy the newspapers, from there we went into the town and he was able to have another lot of sweets in Woolworths, and from there we went on to McDonalds and he could choose two items off the menu. Occasionally Gemma came because of school holidays or something like that. I can tell you that Gemma has never forgotten the fact that when she came she could only have one item from McDonalds, whereas Jamie always had two. What she didn't realise was that my whole life I've been governed by targets and budgets and schedules, and there was a budget for the Friday morning outing! However there is another story to be told with Gemma and Jamie. Gemma was playing at school in a netball game and I can tell you she was a ferocious player. We were all going to watch her play so I had made rosettes from toilet paper and we were making a lot of noise from the sidelines. In fact I heard later that Jamie's teacher commented to Jackie that she now knew where he had learned his mischievous ways.

We settled into Elizabeth House very quickly. The warden, Judith, turned Elizabeth House into what one could only call an extremely happy family, people of all types. Mummie and I were on the young side but we fell in to the organisation and Judith relied quite heavily on both of us to help her with the effort and spirit required to make Elizabeth House a place that everyone could enjoy. We got to know not only those who were residents but their families as well. Certainly at our Christmas parties it was a full house of residents and their families. In fact one Christmas party I must admit we had a band playing which did make a little bit of a racket and at two o'clock in the morning people in Chapel Street rang the police complaining about the noise! How times change.

Mummie and I used to holiday from time to time at Walton on the Naze and we thought it was a good idea to buy a caravan and a beach hut there, as they had very nice sandy beaches and everything that any family would require to have a nice family holiday. Jackie and Jamie came with us to have a look at what was on offer and, true to form, Mummie said that she would settle on the beach and look after Jamie and Jackie and I could go and have a look round to see what there was available. Jackie and I went onto this caravan site which had lots of caravans on it and some were for sale, and we decided there and then which one it was that we would hope to purchase. You can see from the photographs that it was more like a mobile home than a caravan, the sort of place you could live in for days on end without any

Mummie and the mobile home at Walton

bother or fuss. It had two bedrooms, hot and cold running water with a shower, inside toilet, a nice kitchen, a very nice, fairly large and comfortable living room and a veranda all the way round the outside. You can see that from the photographs that it was very suitable for any family to have a holiday in. The purchase went through very smoothly and we were then the proud owners of a mobile home.

Christopher, Lesley, Clive and Simon staying at Walton

Same mobile home with Martin and Ann

The purchase of the beach hut actually came some few months later, certainly within the same first year that we were in Elizabeth House. We came across it by chance, walking along the promenade towards the Naze, which I have to say is most probably the very best part of Walton. It was not in the best condition but it was up for sale and the name of the lady who would be contacted was there so we went to her address straight away and initiated the purchase. It was a nice size beach hut and it held a cooker and a sink and everything that you required to be able to stay there. In fact you could have slept in the hut, although the council disapproved of that but there were some people who did sleep there at weekends. We didn't because we had the caravan. John Fellowes and his brother Kelvin came down and helped tremendously with putting on a new roof and quite a lot of work to put the beach hut into a state in which one could be proud of owning it. This all took time but eventually it was all painted and renovated and looked a very nice beach hut to settle into.

Mummie and me with Martin at the beach hut

131

John and Jackie

Matthew fishing

We made the most of it. We stayed in the caravan, and used the beach hut every day. We very quickly made friends with our neighbours in the beach

132

Life was perfect!

Jamie on the right with friends

huts. We had the caravan and beach hut some ten or twelve years I think, and there was hardly a weekend that would go by in the summer without some of our family or friends being there too, as we enjoyed their company very much indeed.

In the spring of 1988 I started to become quite breathless as I was walking up the steps or stairs or any kind of slope really. I didn't feel unwell and I didn't have pain or anything like that, but I was definitely breathless and so I went to the doctor. He thought it was my age and that really there didn't appear to be very much wrong with me at all. However, I still became breathless, in fact I became somewhat more breathless than I had previously, so I went back to the doctor and asked to see a specialist. He was a little reluctant but never the less he did fix an appointment for me to see a specialist at the West Herts Hospital.

The specialist, Dr Baylis, did treat me very well. He gave me the normal sort of ECG and one or two other tests and blood tests and he more or less told me the same sort of thing. There didn't appear to be anything wrong but he said, 'Well I don't expect to find anything, but I'll give you the bike test – we put you on a bike and monitor you when you're exercising on the bike.' So I went and had this bike test.

Mummie came with me and I had all these wires attached to me and I got on the bike. The specialist was looking at a monitor. I started to pedal as fast as I could and I was definitely breathing extremely uncomfortably at that time, when he shouted, 'Stop, stop, stop!' He asked me, 'How are you feeling?'

'Yeah, well I'm OK.'

'Do you know according to this monitor, you should be dead on the floor?'

'Oh dear.'

'What we'll do is you'll have to come in to the hospital straight away.'

I said, 'Well I've got my car here, I'll take my wife home and then ...'

'No, no, no, no, no!' he said. 'We'll lift you off the bike and we'll put you on the stretcher and you'll have to come into the hospital onto a ward straight away.'

I couldn't believe it at the time although I remember thinking well I knew there was something which wasn't right. Anyway Mummie had to make arrangements for someone to come and pick my car up and of course at the same time to pick her up when she was ready to go. As I was being carried into the ward the sister met me at the door and said, 'Oh here's the miracle man.'

A specialist came and saw me, and apparently he had worked under Professor Yakoub, who as you most probably know is the man who appears on television and talks about heart operations, and is one of the top men I would imagine in the whole world when it comes to heart operations. He fixed it for me to have the angiogram at the National Heart Hospital and they found was that one of my arteries was totally blocked and two of them were fifty per cent blocked and so that it was now just a question of having a bypass operation and fixing that up. He was able to get me onto Professor Yakoub's list, which was very fortunate but I would have to wait some two or three months for that to happen He said as long as I rested and took things very easy indeed there was no need for any sort of problems, I would be perfectly all right in that time providing I did what he said and that was to rest. I could drive but only very short distances and going to the caravan was quite out of the question.

Anyway the two or three months went by and I had the letter to be taken to the National Heart Hospital to have a heart bypass. Fortunately my sister lives very close to the hospital and so Mummie was able to stay with her and come backwards and forwards to the hospital as opposed to coming home all the time to Elizabeth House. On the Monday, I was going to have the operation on the Tuesday, I had to do something extremely difficult and that was to shave off all the hairs that were on my body apart from the hair on my head. I have always been quite a hairy sort of person so it took some time and a couple of nurses or so to finish the job off, but we did it. Then came the Tuesday and I was now ready for the operation. Another specialist came down to see me and tell me that Professor Yakoub would perform the operation. So I lay on the trolley and away I went.

Come the evening time, I was now back in the bed. Mummie had come to see me and she said, 'How do you feel?' I said, 'Yeah I feel all right, it's not what I expected at all.' Then she broke the news that I hadn't had the operation. I was last on the list and the man before me took very much longer than expected, in fact he died while he was under and therefore my operation was cancelled. Along came the Sister who told me to go home and they would make another appointment. I told her quite plainly that I was not getting out of this bed until such time that I'd had the operation. She went quiet and got another nurse, and after some discussion they went away and came back and said, 'Well, we are going to allow you to stay here until you have the operation next Tuesday. Professor Yakoub only operates on a Tuesday.'

I stayed in the bed, in the ward. Fortunately for me I was quite well really, but there were all these poor men who were coming in after their operations, feeling very depressed and sorry for themselves. I tried to keep up the morale of the ward and the Sister was very pleased. She said, 'This is normally a very depressing ward but you certainly have put a bit of spark of life into it.'

Then came my turn. I was then in intensive care for two or three days and

I know that John Fellowes, Jackie's husband, came to see me. When he saw all the wires coming out of me, he collapsed, and so having come to cheer me up he was a total calamity. He remembers it quite well. I can tell you that it's a sort of operation that does tend to depress people but I tried to keep my spirits up. Next to me was a television set and in the next bed was an Italian, something to do with the Italian embassy in London. My brother-in-law came and took photographs of me in the bed and when he'd gone, the Italian was obviously trying to find out what the photograph was all about. I led him along that I was a television star; I mimed a guitar and a mike, and pointed at the television set. He must have thought I was some sort of television celebrity because he went and got his book out for me to sign my name.

I came home, I think it was earlier than seven days. I was told to rest, to exercise but to rest. On the day that I was leaving, I had to say goodbye to the nurse and the Sister and she said, 'Thank you very much for entertaining us.' I said, 'Oh there will be someone else come along,' and she said, 'Well, there is only one John Skelton.' I thought that was rather nice of her to say that, I think she was just trying to keep my spirits up.

I can tell you that it was a depressing time but Mummie looked after me wonderfully well. She was just one of those patient people and knew just how I was feeling. I think I did say once to her that I did think I was never

Operation over!

136

going to feel well again and it rather shook her that I was feeling in that sort of mood. However, we got through the Christmas, because my operation was actually on 2 November 1988. Life started to get better again. I was doing my exercises and I was going to rehabilitation classes and slowly but surely things were improving.

In February 1989 we went on a Saga holiday to Lloret de Mar and I felt that going away was the completion of my convalescence. We then started our weekly journeys to Walton again which always started in the first week of April until the first week of September. We used to leave Elizabeth House on Thursday mornings, returning the following Tuesday morning leaving us just Tuesday afternoons and Wednesdays in Elizabeth house. We were always having people stay, family and friends also some of our friends from Elizabeth House from time to time. George and his wife came two or three times and we always remember the story of how I was going to throw a transistor radio into the sea because it was being played far too loud next to us, by a couple of teenagers who refused to turn it down. They knew I meant business when I picked it up and went down to the sea to throw the set into the sea, however they simply just left. George and I became good friends. I used to take him to see Arsenal play their home games, and we had our scarves and a hat etc., and stood in the same place at every game. I can tell you that we were vocal supporters and at a time when the away supporters mixed with the home supporters, from time to time we caused a bit of trouble. Once we got trapped between two police horses, what a palaver that was – goodness only knows you've never seen anybody in such a state. Happy times though, we enjoyed our pint of Guinness in the George Roby before we went into the game. It got us ready for the fun of the afternoon.

We had some very good neighbours at the beach hut. Next door to us were Bill and Ivy and next door to them was Pat. It was a real community, and they got to know our family very well and we also got to know their family. We mixed together on the sand and there's no doubt that they were extremely happy days for us all.

Mummie and I made a conscious decision that in our retirement it was going to be all about us. We just felt that we had done 'our bit' and for the rest of our lives together we would do what we both enjoyed doing. That was to be together, travel and have fun, and I can assure you we did just that. Of course events from time to time had to be overcome but I only know that when the end came, we were just as much in love with each other as we were on our wedding day. Just before she died, Mummie wrote a letter to a friend who sent me a quote from it, and you have to remember that we had been married over sixty-five years: 'John is a wonderful person and a wonderful husband. He was the same person who got up in the morning and stayed the same throughout the whole day. He always made me very happy and I never want to be without him.'

The start of our retirement was the purchase of the mobile home and the beach hut, knowing that both of us loved seaside holidays with family and friends. We were now going to go further afield. Not that we hadn't been abroad previously, we had, but we were able to go more often. We had no intention of taking any sort of part time jobs or joining any clubs etc. It was just going to be Mummie and me, and we were going to enjoy this retirement that we had worked for so many years to enjoy.

16

In December 1989 my mother died. She was a frail person towards the end and her mind was not the same as it really was in her earlier years. She died at home, she collapsed. My sister was very quickly there and she took over the running of the funeral arrangements. We all went to the funeral, including Roland which I was very pleased about, even though he knew that the split of the family was over decisions that he had made some few years earlier.

Mother had no money, it was a question of us burying her and the family joined in. However, Granny Murray isn't really gone. Whenever the Skeltons get together, and even today it's still exactly the same, it will not be long before Granny Murray's name comes up – what she did and what she said and how she acted and that she was a formidable person, without any shadow of a doubt, whether you went along with her views or not. Later on in her life, she said she had come to the view that no matter which colour of government was in power, what made a difference to the way in which ordinary people lived was the decisions that they made themselves. So she passed that on to me. She was quite right that if you look at your own life it's all been about what you've decided to do and certainly not what other people have decided that you should do.

As I have already said, we only spent one and a half days a week in Elizabeth House in the summer. While we were in Walton we travelled around the Suffolk area with our family and friends which included going to where I was born, in Felixstowe. Only a short time ago George said to me that he remembers the time that he spoke about going to the house that I was born in and looking in the back garden etc. We often went to Harwich and Dovercourt, as many of Peggy's cousins live there and she used to spend her summer holidays with her mother and father at Dovercourt. Some of the photographs of Peggy and her mother were taken at Dovercourt when she was about fourteen years old. Another favourite place was Flatford Mill, which of course is in Constable country, where he painted the famous Haywain picture. Martin and Anne liked Flatford Mill and walked along the river to Debden which had some very quaint old fashioned shops.

At Elizabeth House we joined in all the games and parties, which both Peggy and I helped to organise. I organised the famous gang show, and

The special young lady who I was privileged to marry

'Please come home safely, I am all yours'

Peggy, myself and Ann walking at Flatford Mill

I've now got one of them on a DVD which I show to people who are interested in what went on during that time. We did six shows in all, over those years, and one show we did at the Pavilion, where there were a couple of thousand or so people in the audience. It was great fun but very hard work.

The Gang Show

The Pukka Chicken

More fun

Mummie enjoying herself in both photos. She was a star!

In February of each year of our first six years of retirement we went to Benidorm to a hotel called The Calypso, and of course we met the same people year after year and made a few friends such as Mary and Danny from Oldham and many others. The routine at The Calypso was the same every day; we would get up and have breakfast and then we would walk along the promenade. We would arrive back around about twelve o'clock to a little bar which was close to The Calypso where we met many of our friends. We would be there for about an hour or so and then go over to The Calypso for our lunch, we were on full board.

The food at The Calypso was excellent and nobody ever complained about either the quality or the quantity. Peggy and I would then go up to our room and fortunately for us, after the first year or two, we always had the same room on the sunny side of the hotel in the afternoon and we were able to sit out on the veranda for an hour or so. Then we would go to bed, get up around about five o'clock or just after, have a shower and get ourselves ready for the evening, going downstairs around about seven o'clock. We used to place our coats and belongings on a table in the front row of the ballroom and then go down to have our evening meal. We would come back from the evening well in time for the first dance which was always around the eight o'clock time. Mary and Danny were always there with us and other friends would be there. Mummie and I we'd just dance, we never missed the first dance and every dance right up until such time it was over round about half past eleven. Peggy was not able to keep up with my energy and so there were times when I had to have different partners, but only because she'd always had difficulty with dancing the foxtrot and so I was able to always have a foxtrot with some other dancer. I never missed one dance; I kept going all the time. Then when it finished Peggy and I went on to a nightclub every night. We would dance until about two or two thirty and then go back to the hotel.

You'll now understand why it was that we needed that sleep in the afternoon to keep us going because we did that for twenty eight days, every day! We were sitting on the promenade one day and two sisters came along and sat down beside us, like we always used to do, and started talking. One of them said, 'You're the dancer in the blue shirt aren't you?' I said 'Well I don't know if I always wear a blue shirt but I wear a blue shirt on occasion so yes, I do dance quite a lot.' She said, 'My sister would love to have a dance with you, perhaps one of these times that you are dancing with other people you might give her a dance.' I said 'Yes I would, where do you sit?' Eventually I did give her sister a dance, she wasn't a great dancer but she was able to go home and tell her friends that one evening she'd had a dance with a man with a blue shirt. You can imagine that by the end of twenty-eight days we were exhausted and therefore March was one of the months in which we relaxed. We still mixed in with whatever was going on in Elizabeth House but we had a much quieter time in March, and got ready then for our journey to Walton from April.

In Elizabeth House we had a magazine. It was not monthly in fact, in the ten years or so that it was published in the house we certainly did thirty issues. It's the best way to put across to you what it was like in Elizabeth House, and you can read a part which was put in by the co-editor of the magazine in one of the issues. I must say that he did miss out some activities such as the monthly dancing lessons, the bingo and the auctions of which I used to be the auctioneer selling items other residents no longer required. Great fun. However you can get a feel of the type of residents and the type of activity that went on in Elizabeth House in those first ten years by reading what Frank has to say.

A DECADE WITH "THE ELIZABETHAN"

No.1 Issue - AUG. 1987
No.30 " - JUNE 1997

Being involved with the Magazine from the start, I have saved a copy of all editions from No.1 onwards.
So I've been having another look at these old magazines to see what was happening in the ten years.

We certainly seemed to have been very energetic in the early days, in fact I can remember somebody remarking we were "having a second childhood"!

For instance, the first edition records in the 'Social Diary Dates', A Mystery Tour Leaving 7 PM, Learn to Paint lessons in the lounge, a stall in Hemel market and a London by Night Tour, to mention just a few of the activities. Then in the 2nd Issue I notice we were having a 'VE Night' Celebration, with all drinks at 1945 prices, followed by the 'Elizabeth House Gang', a great entertainment put on by our tenants themselves.

In Issue 4 I see we record the 'Elizabeth House Gang' at the Pavilion. They were actually singing and dancing there and doing comedy acts such as Flannaghan & Allen and Soft Shoe shuffles!

Issue 4 saw the start of a serial, the story of tenant Tony Lewis's life (flat 103). It went on until Issue 8 and surprisingly interesting it was too, (though hard work typing it out). No more to say about this except to mention that at 3 months Tony was so poorly that the doctor despaired and told his parents to prepare for the worst!

And what about the Town Carnivals, I see Issue 5 describes the great efforts put into our float in the summer of 1988 and our tableau winning 2nd prize in Cl.II, a useful £20. The following year we entered the Town Carnival again, the theme was Eastern. We had harem girls, sheiks, a snake charmer, a big gong, palm trees and a huge blown up snake. Again after a great procession through crowds in the town we ended up in Gadebridge Park being presented with another prize by the Mayor.

Issue 15 describes the Old High Street celebrations of the Charter being granted to the town 500 years ago by the King, Henry 8th. 32 stalls, including ours, were selling anything you could imagine, old time street entertainers and an Elizabethan Band were there, also our Jock made up marvellously as Henry 8th. The bells of St.Mary's rang out for a wedding and the BBC people were getting the church wired up ready for their Songs of Praise programme.

Issue 17 records the sum of £545.52 being raised for Macmillan Nurses and the cheque for that sum being handed to the Mayor at coffee morning on 27th May 1992.
Something to be proud of.

....the Mayor was/

-5-

146

A DECADE - Cont'd
_____

The Mayor came again last October, with his Lady,
to judge our Arts & Crafts show. This was another
memorable Coffee Morning.

Space only allows me to touch briefly on events at
Elizabeth House during the ten years its been open.
So much more has been going on and the magazines
(now up to No.30) have recorded it all, including
parties, outings, stories, poems, jokes, puzzles
and, of course, many many Recipes.

May the complex of flats we know as Elizabeth House
go on with its comfortable and peaceful provision
of homes for its tenants, for another good decade.

                                        Frank.

I can only say after reading about that decade in the *Elizabethan*, that Mummie and I, we simply loved each other then, perhaps more than we did when we were first married. We were never apart, we were extremely close, and our sex life was such that it was no different from our early years. I can only say that we would have done anything for each other and if she was writing this story instead of me I'm quite certain that she would be using the same words as I am, and that is that we simply lived for each other and never wanted to be without each other.

After we had done our trips to the Calypso for about six years so, we started to feel that we needed to go a little further afield. We often had a weekend in Paris, and we would just decide almost on the spur of the moment to go. We loved Paris, we loved walking around the city, we loved the Louvre and Montmartre and the walk down at the Cours la Reine and of course Notre Dame was a favourite place for us to go. We went a couple of times to Malta, and to Rome and Majorca and several other places.

We had to deal with one or two things which were happening at home. The first was that Lesley went back to live in Scotland. Her husband was transferred with his job from where he was working to Prestwick and they got a house in East Kilbride, the same town that Mummie and I lived in and Lesley had lived in in the earlier years. The other occurrence was the sad break-up temporarily of Jackie and John's marriage. I'm pretty certain it was in 1994 and it came out of the blue to us, as we were not privy to anything which had gone on, we only knew that John was leaving the house. It was shortly after they had moved into Sandpit Lane, where the idea was that they would extend the house and work had been put in hand. The break-up was for several months. It now meant that Mummie and I did quite a lot of work in the house with doing the garden and keeping it tidy and doing the washing up and all the other sorts of things which would help Jackie because she was still going to work. Her friends, Pat and Colin helped a lot, and what great friends they were and have remained great friends ever since. It started a friendship between Pat and Peggy and myself. Pat was showing me how to do the tiling and wallpapering and lots of other jobs which I'd never done in my life before – the joke was that you could always find Pat and me banging away on the floor in the bedroom any time that you called. I learnt to fit floorboards and do skirting.

The timing I can't be absolutely certain about, but there was a reconciliation. It was some months, it could have been a shorter period, it could have been a little longer, but they got back together and they've been together ever since and people will know that it was all a big mistake. They have been very happy together ever since.

Of course we were still going to our mobile home and the beach hut on a regular basis, in fact in the end we did that for some twelve years. We decided that we'd like to go to America and we went on a fourteen-day coach trip which was to cover the west coast, that is from San Francisco, Santa Barbara, Palm Springs and up to Las Vegas. I think I can safely say for both of us that it was probably the best holiday we had. It was hard work in as much that we were up every morning quite early and taken here there and everywhere. In San Francisco we went to Alcatraz, over to the island itself and round the prison. We had a phone set with us telling us exactly where we were and what was going on and one of the frightening parts was when we came to the Birdman's cell. The message was to go into the cell and then the door shuts. I can assure you that Mummie thought she was in there for a lifetime. You will be surprised to know that the story of the Birdman of Alcatraz was not quite true; there was a man in another prison who was looking after birds in his cell but according to what we were told on the phone he didn't actually ever have any birds while he was in Alcatraz.

We went to Santa Barbara, a very nice place indeed, and Palm Springs, from there we had a wagon trip out into the desert. Then we arrived in Las Vegas. We were housed in one of the biggest hotels in Las Vegas – three or four thousand rooms. We did the normal things one does in Las Vegas, we were only there for three or four days but we did the casinos and the bright lights and saw the shows which were put on by the hotels that are free of charge. Of course being on a coach tour the people who were in charge knew what time we could expect a show for quarter of an hour, twenty minutes purely and simply to get you into a hotel and they would put them on at the same time each day and so the tour operator knew exactly where to take us in order that we covered anything that was needed to be covered. We then had the famous aircraft trip through the Grand Canyon; I can assure you that it is something that will stay with you for the rest of your life.

One of the things that did happen on the trip on the coach was that the travel company were celebrating their twenty-fifth year of operations so in each American trip they were giving a free weekend holiday in Paris for somebody on each coach. There was a draw and the person who was in charge picked a name out of the hat. It was someone from Hemel Hempstead. Mummie turned to me and said, 'Oh fancy that, there's someone else on the coach who comes from Hemel Hempstead, we hadn't noticed that.' But then of course the lady said, 'And it is Mr and Mrs John Skelton.' The lady who was sitting across the aisle from us said, 'Well you're not going to accept that are you?' I said, 'Of course we are.' She said, 'But you've been to Paris many times. Why don't you give it to somebody who's never been to Paris?' I couldn't understand how someone could have the nerve to even suggest that I would give that away, and if that lady reads this story, I can tell you we did have the weekend in Paris, it was very nice indeed.

We enjoyed the whole experience, so we decided that the next year we would do it ourselves, fly to San Francisco and stay in San Francisco for I think it was six or seven days and then we would fly on to Las Vegas. And we did and we stayed in Las Vegas for six or seven days and then we came back home. So we had done that trip twice, we enjoyed every minute of it and I can recommend to anybody that if you see a trip like that being advertised then take advantage of it.

I must now show you some photographs of this particular American trip, of course we have plenty to choose from but I thought that there were several that you would like to see to confirm what I've been telling you. Mummie's favourite is the one which shows her playing the grand piano in the Marriott Hotel in Palm Springs. Through the whole of her life she wanted a grand piano and unfortunately it was one of those things which we could never get round to, pure and simply because in the first place we never had the finance to do it and when we did have we didn't have conditions which were suitable for a grand piano.

Locked in at Alcatraz

Riding through the outback at Palm Springs

The Hollywood sign

At last – a grand piano!

The Grand Canyon

The Grand Canyon

Waiting to fly through the Canyon

MR.FIESTA   1997

I am writing this story to show you that life has not necessarily passed you by at 70 plus.

On a recent holiday in Majorca we went to a Complex with mixed age groups and the over 60's in the minority. We had two very good young men in charge of activities, who were always on the look out for people to enter their competitions.

John agreed to enter the Mr.Fiesta competition the Complex belonging to Fiesta Hotels.

We were told that it had nothing to do with age, appearance etc but was based entirely on one's ability to carry out certain tasks in games. They needed 5 contestants, and John was Number 4.

The first assignment was that each person had to stand erect with arms extended sideways at shoulder level and hold a bucket of sand in each hand for as long as possible. As soon as one shoulder dropped, the contestant was out.   The first contestant was a lad about 22 years of age, dressed for the part in the latest fashion, who thought he was sure to do well. As he raised the buckets the audience started to count 1- 2- 3 etc and he went out at 32 seconds.
NO.2 was a good looking, young, sturdy man of about 26 years of age, and he raised the buckets and went out at 40 odd.
NO.3 was a man of similar age and he was out for about the same score. By this time, John was thinking 'I don't know how I'm going to get on, so the only thing I can do is to relax'. The others had been very tense and looked in agony. He stood up straight, held the buckets up and relaxed. The counting started, and when he had passed the totals of the others, the noise started to increase. At fifty, they were roaring and shouting, and at sixty, the roof was nearly coming off and he finally got to 68 seconds to thunderous applause and shouting. Next came contestant NO 5 a man of about 50 years of age, and we later found out that he was a miner. The count started and the roars began at forty plus, building up at fifty plus, but although he looked so strong he went out at 54 seconds. So John was the winner and the applause was deafening, putting the crowd on his side from then onwards. I will never know how he did it, for it was not an easy thing to do, and a bit humiliating for the much younger men to be beaten by an older man. The winner of each game collected 25 points. Runner up 20 points, third 15 and so on.

NO 2 GAME Everyone was given a bottle of beer with a straw to drink as fast as possible - John was a close second. The crowd encouraged everyone there was a lot of shouting, and calling going on.
The third was a General Knowledge Competition, I think he was probably second in this.
The next task was to choose a person of character of one's own choice, and find a member of the audience who they thought resembled that person. John chose Marilyn Munroe because there was a blond girl watching and the nearest look alike he could see. Someone c use Mavis Rilet etc. etc.

............./Contd........

The next game each contestant was given a female to follow them
around the room to count how many ladies the man could kiss in two
minutes.   John was first with 28, the runner up 25.   It was then
half time so that the contestants had the opportunity for a drink
if they wished.

For the next half, four lady judges were chosen to vote on the performance of each contestant giving 25 for their first choice, twenty
for their second etc.
This time the men had to be Tarzan in a leopard skin costume and
everyone else rolled up their trousers and kept their socks on. But
of course John did not, he took off his trousers, shoes and socks,
for who can swim a river with clothes on !   This got a big roar and
wolf whistles !   They had to swim the lake, kill a crocodile and
rescue Jane.   The crocodile an inflatable, was thrown on to the stage
which I found very amusing because for fifty years John had been
telling our sons and later our grandchildren, how he killed the
crocodile and won a medal from the Queen.   In fact in our flat we
have a small crocodile presented to him on his 70th birthday by a
grandson in recognition of all the story telling.   So obviously after
all that practice he knew exactly what to do - and went down a storm.

Next each participant was asked to mime a pop star or personality.
The music was chosen for them by the entertainment lads and the costumes
John got The Village People and Y.M.C.A.   He was given a leather
brimmed hat and leather waistcoat and kerchief, and with hat over one
eye he strutted his stuff up and down the stage.   By now all the
teenagers were roaring and whistling for him too, it was deafening.
Good job he didn't get Prince or Queen, he would have been out of his
depth.

Last of all was an interview when everyone was asked what they would do
if they won £1 million pounds.   Most people said they would buy a house
and car, go on holiday etc but John said he would have no problem with
four children and ten grandchildren they would spend it for him.

The last event everyone was given a slip of five numbers from 1 - 5
and had to tear off the number of the contestant of their choice and
put it in a bucket.   The judges marks were added up with the numbers
in the bucket, and the result was that the runner up received 410 votes
and John received 630.   When he was asked to say a few words, he said
thank you to all his supporters, he had never expected to win as he was
73 years old.   The applause and cheering was deafening, and one
wondered how he could beat all those younger men so convincingly.
The entertainment men said then, that for the remainder of his
holiday he was never to be known by his own name, but must be called
Mr.Fiesta at all times.   Everyone was supposed to bow down to him,
and many did too, especially the children who thought he was Superman
after the bucket competition.   But it did win us many friends and it
was very nice that so many young people came and chatted to us.
As new comers came, you could see people with out stretched arms
explaining what had happened.

The icing on the cake came when one of the younger contestants came
to us on the night before he left to go home and told John that he
thought he deserved to know what he had beaten.   He said he was a

/Cond.................

-10-

154

Third Black Belt Karate expert, and had expected to do well in that event. He said he had always believed in the power of the mind and that he now was a true believer in Mind over Matter and utterly convinced after seeing what someone so much older could do.

After that evening Mr.Fiesta could do no wrong and went on to win the Supremes Backing Group Competition, the Yes No Competition and got to the finals of the Generation Game.

In all he won 17 prizes, several free drinks free meals, 5 bottles of Champagne a Tee Shirt and a Fiesta Badge plus 2 Certificates to hang in the Beach Hut with which to entertain the children.

I must admit to being very proud of his performance in beating such younger men in view of his past Medical History, it was an amazing experience to everyone present. Considering too that the previous week Miss Fiesta won by a margin of 5 Votes.

So ladies, never give up !!!

Peggy 211

.   .   .   .   .

For the rest of the holiday Peggy held my hand the gesture being. Mr Fiesta is not available he is all mine!!

The crowning of Mr Fiesta

155

In 1994 we had our fiftieth wedding anniversary party. Fifty years go by quite quickly and as you can well imagine the family organised a big do. There were relatives, friends and all the ingredients that go to make a good party. Plenty of singing and dancing and speeches and everything went according to plan. We didn't realise then that there was still the sixtieth and the sixty-fifth to come. I'm just showing you two photographs, one is of Mummie and me and the other is the wedding cake. As you can see she was dressed in a gold suit, and didn't she look absolutely lovely.

Another reminder of a special person

I'm going to go further forward now to the early part of 1996 – it could have been late '95 but I'm fairly certain it was the early part of '96 – when we went to Dijon in France. We lived as students did, as we were staying with Sophie and her friend in their student house. This friend was studying French law. There were other students in the same house and we mixed in with them and Sophie showed us along with the other students how students lived in their student days. I can assure you that it was an eye opener to both Mummie and myself but I understand that the way they were living was the accepted way for students. I think the one thing which surprised me more than anything else was Sophie saying, 'When you go to the toilet while you're out make certain you always bring some toilet paper home because there will always be a time or so when you go to the toilet in the house and there will be no toilet paper there.' You could multiply those sentiments many times but we lived like them, we enjoyed being young. We enjoyed the company of the students, they were absolutely great; we have seen several of them since then and it is one of the things which we've talked about many times.

In 1996 we were privileged to go to Sophie's graduation ceremony, when she received a first class honours degree in law from Manchester. We were very kindly invited by Roz and Alistair who paid all the expenses of the three days and we were extremely thankful for what they did. We travelled up there, we had a good time, as you can see from the photographs the weather was not all that great but that didn't bother us. Sophie was fortunate in as much as she was able to get two tickets for the ceremony so we were not only honoured by being there and having the celebration meal afterwards but we were able to be at the ceremony itself.

Myself, Peggy and Roz – away in not very good weather

Proud Sophie

No caption is necessary

It was about this time when Peggy's arthritis started to be somewhat more painful than previously. She'd had it for some time and had never really complained, we'd just continued doing what we'd liked doing. As it was getting somewhat more painful there was a question of going to the doctors and finding some sort of treatment for her. I think she was given some tablets, probably more painkillers than anything else. However she was also having some bowel trouble and they diagnosed this as irritable bowel syndrome. The diagnoses was followed with, 'Well what you should do is just find out those foods which do upset you and cause this diarrhoea, and not eat it at all.' Not a very satisfactory situation but that was how it was left and left for some time. I can tell you it didn't stop us, we had made up our minds and we were just having fun and we were going to go on having fun.

We went on a trip, I think this was about 1998, to Holland, an organised trip but we stayed in a private house. It was a small seaside town called Katwijk and we had bed and breakfast with a very nice couple who lived right on the seafront. We had our evening meal organised by the tour operator that we were with in a hotel. They were lovely people. Further, we were there at the fiftieth anniversary of the liberation of Holland, I can tell you that that night it was absolutely hectic. I've never been kissed and cuddled so many times in my life ... what a night, a night to remember. We went to see the tulip fields and the famous garden in Holland, Keukenhof, a wonderful place to see. It was absolutely magnificent. We went to Amsterdam and went into the famous Anne Frank house.

We also went to Paris once again because we always seemed to be in Paris at one time or another, but this was in the time that Paris was holding the World Cup and so I thought I'd just show you a photograph of Peggy mixing in with some of the supporters of one of the World Cup teams.

The World Cup in Paris

Of course there were other trips. We went to Rome and went into the Sistine Chapel and stood in the square where the Pope gives his message but the emotional part for us was when we went from Rome to Monte Casino. Monte Casino in the war was a place where hundreds upon hundreds of soldiers lost their lives in trying to take this monastery from the Germans who had fortified it at the top of a fairly large mountain. The Americans in the end bombed it, bombed it absolutely to smithereens. After the war it was reconstructed into the same space as it was before the bombing, and Mummie and I went there. From the time that we got off the coach there was absolutely total silence, there were quite a few people there but no one said anything. It had an effect on both of us and we did talk about it and we often wondered about those people who had connections there. Just exactly what they would have been feeling while they were going through this terrible atrocity.

I must tell you just one more little story of holiday, I can't remember if this was in Tenerife or Majorca, it was one of those places, where we met two Irish people, Liam and Sarah McGuire. They lived and had a bed and breakfast in I think it was Letterkenny in County Donegal and they had a daughter who was about thirteen. We sat with them around the pool most days, the girl had a friend much about the same age, and we talked and talked. The young girl who was the friend, her mother and father came over once or twice, and they said to us that they were hiring a car the next day to go out and see more of the island and the young girl and the daughter would be coming with them. However the next day came and the young girl turned up beside the pool. We said to her, 'We thought you were going away with your parents?' and she said, 'No, I'd rather sit and listen to John's stories than be sitting in the car.' I thought that was rather nice.

Anyway, we told Liam and Sarah that we would come and stay with them in their bed and breakfast, and we did. I can't remember what year, all I know is that we didn't actually have what would be a normal bed and breakfast. We didn't sit in the guest room part of the house we actually sat in the kitchen with them and had our meals with them. Liam took us around in his car and showed us all the sights that needed to be seen in that part of Ireland. A wonderful time. We exchanged Christmas cards with them for a very long time but somehow or other it got broken off and while I still have their address in the address book I don't know whether they would still be alive.

We sold the caravan and the beach hut in 1999. We had had them some twelve years and it was our intention now to travel even more. Those people in Elizabeth House never knew when we were actually going away next or when we were there. It was all 'So where are you going next?' and 'Where have you just come back from?' We were well known for travelling around not only abroad but also around the UK. We went to Ilfracome quite a few times and Woolacombe Bay was one of our very favourite spots. The Lake District and the Derbyshire Dales too, and we walked around York many times. Plus we used to have an annual week's holiday in a caravan in Weymouth, a very nice place indeed. In Weymouth harbour is a fish and chip shop which sells, without a shadow of a doubt, the best fish and chips you'll taste anywhere in the UK. We were still travelling abroad as well and there were very few seaside resorts right around the east coast, west coast and south coast that we had not visited.

It was coming up the time for the millennium and I can remember that we had the party to beat all parties. It was held in Portsmouth, we were all in fancy dress. It was a typical Skelton party and I'm not sure what time it stopped. It was a rip-roaring time and those who went there and stayed relatively sober will be able to tell you more about the party than I can. But it was one of those parties which we have many photographs of and many happy memories of that millennium night.

17

It was about this time, 2000 to 2001, that Peggy's stomach problem became a great deal worse and she had some tests, in fact one was a biopsy. It wasn't irritable bowel syndrome that she had, she was actually a sufferer of coeliac disease. Coeliac disease is a disease of the bowel which is activated eating anything which contains gluten and therefore from that moment onwards she had to have a gluten free diet. In those days in the supermarkets and places like that very little was known about coeliac disease or gluten free food, and a great deal of it was not marked. So for quite a long time it was extremely difficult for us to make certain that we were not buying or eating anything which contained gluten. I know that there were a few members of the family who rather felt that it was more of a fad than a disease, but I can assure you that it certainly was no fad at all because if Mummie ate anything that contained gluten then certainly half way to the toilet she would be caught and it would be rather nasty.

Anything which is fresh, vegetables and meat and fresh fruits and those sorts of things is perfectly OK. It's when it starts to be processed or manufactured that gluten comes into the problem. I'll tell you how strange things are and that is that you can buy black pepper; some of it is gluten free and some of it isn't. Crisps; some are gluten free, some are not. Even vinegar; some is gluten free, some is not. It's not an easy thing to get used to. It did mean that our whole lifestyle was changed. Eating out these days of course many restaurants do have a gluten free menu but in those early years there was no such thing. It wasn't a common thing for people to be diagnosed with coeliac disease. Many, many more now are diagnosed. There is a Coeliac Society, which Mummie joined, and they would produce a book year by year from the supermarkets to show which of their foods were gluten free and which were not.

Mummie was still determined that it wasn't going to interfere with our social life or our party life; she could still cut a rug and she was determined that life would still be a ball. It was. She did get annoyed with those people who thought she was too fussy about the diet and anything that she was eating, but she knew the embarrassment that could be caused by any mistake that was made. Lesley herself will remember the time that when we were once in Blackpool and Mummie ate something late at night before she went to bed, and that it wasn't long during the night before a mess was created down the hallway and into the toilets. It's not a pleasant subject to write about, but I want people to know that when someone says that they suffer from coeliac disease, the business of only wanting to eat gluten free food is not a fad at all, it is absolute reality that that is what they must eat.

Once we'd moved to Elizabeth House, we had to give up holding the family Christmas parties which had always been a feature of the whole of our lives really. Jackie and John held some legendary Boxing Day parties where there were always thirty plus people and certainly there was no question of a television set being on. We played lots and lots of games, they were the same games year after year, I used to have the names of the people who were going to be at the party and I'd draw up a playing list for each game: bowls, darts, dominos, connect four, etc., etc. There were always about eight games or so. I used to arrange the games and play a bookmaker and people who wanted to bet on any particular person to win either a game or to win a final I was always there for them to be able place their bets. It was all quite fun, there was no great amount of money in it but it did make those things very interesting. Mummie and I went round the family, you can't always be in the same place.

I remember two parties in particular where I think the first was held at Martin's house and they did much the same thing, ie, the television was off and games would be played. I remember one particular party that had a golf game where you had to put the ball down the stairs. So it went down the stairs, along the carpet and into the hole. You do have to remember that the people who were there were golfers, and one was a golf professional, but who got the hole in one with the putt down the stairs? It was dear old granddad. It was not met with applause; it was met with almost silence other than that one great lady who was shouting her head off for her Dear John, what a marvellous John he was. What you won't believe was the next year when we were at Roland's and it was the same sort of thing and we were playing this particular same golf game, what happened was once again the ball went down the stairs and along the carpet and into the hole. Who got the hole in one? It was granddad again. There was a little bit of clapping, not too much, but with the first one they gave me the golf ball in a cup and presented me with it in the evening and when I did it the second time another cup was produced. On my window ledge at home are these two golf balls, the two golf balls which I got the holes in one with. Nobody could believe it but there it was, this frail old man beating these athletic, professional and very good golfers and I don't think that they have ever forgotten.

Mummie's health was starting to deteriorate somewhat with her arthritis as most people will know, which is a progressive thing. It didn't deter her, she continued to enjoy herself but it did mean that we had to find a place to go that was warm and hot but not humid. It had to be dry, and Spain was recommended so we started to go to Benidorm, to a very nice apartment right on the front. I can't remember the year that we started going there but I do remember the year that Jackie and John and Gemma and Jamie came.

Jackie, John, Gemma and Jamie in our first apartment in Benidorm

Jackie decided that we ought to go to Benidorm more regularly and for a longer period, and so she marched us along to the estate agent to see if there was any other accommodation that we could go to for, say, a month. By the time we came out of the estate agents we had booked into another apartment for the whole of October and we understood that the weather could be very good at that time of the year. The apartment that we would go to for the month was Las Damas, it was rather close to the beach and there was no difficulty with us getting there from the apartment. While we were there we enjoyed all the fun and games of the nightclubs, I don't think there's a nightclub in Benidorm that at some time or another we hadn't been to. All the nightclubs get in professional entertainers and I can tell you some of them were very good; some of them were not as good but the dancing and the atmosphere of the nightclub we thoroughly enjoyed and we went to them most nights of the week.

It did mean that, being self-catering, getting gluten free food in Spain was even more difficult than it was in the UK, and so one of our cases didn't

In love. Still enjoying our wonderful life together

We just loved dancing together

contain very much in the way of clothes just everything we would need in the way of gluten free products. Of course in Spain you can eat a great deal of fresh food and so with the fresh food and the sorts of things that we took from the UK we managed very well. We got used to it, it wasn't easy, but we made very little fuss of it, it had to be done and we did it. It was really only when we went to other people's homes that there was a problem, because we were never really too sure that they were being quite as careful as we were with making sure that nothing got on the plate that in any shape or form had gluten in it.

Mummie felt so much better in the sunshine and dry sort of climate that Spain has to offer that we decided we would go very much more often. We thought about living there full time but we very quickly discarded that idea because we had our family and Elizabeth House and many things that we could continue to do. We decided that we would go for three or four months, and for the next year or so that's what we did in March, June, October and then November although after a time we cut that back to three months. It appeared to do Mummie's arthritis a great deal of good. In the photo of us loading her up to leave the beach you can see that in no way was she an invalid, although those who knew her understood that the arthritis was an extremely painful business for her.

The loaded porter

Being there so often we made some wonderful lifelong friends, one of whom I still keep in touch with. Ann and David McLeod lived close to Edinburgh stayed at Las Damas as well. We used to see them regularly on the beach and they would come into our apartment and we would go into theirs. We didn't meet them socially because by this time our social activities were simply walking along the promenade and just taking in the nice warm sunshine, but we met them during the day and coffee with them. I can tell you that they were two very nice people who helped us out a tremendous amount in the last year or two of our time going to Benidorm. Another two that I should mention are our French friends Roger and Anne-Marie, and they were also quite close to them. We used to have some parties at Las Damas apartments when quite a gang of us all got together and you'll see from the photograph that we used to have a lot of fun and laughter.

While I am talking about the friends we met over the years I must also say a few words about Terrence and Anne. They came from Wales and they were in Benidorm many a month when we were there. Once Terrence was going to give a speech, I think it was at a wedding, and he asked me if I would write it for him, which I did. We used to rehearse it on the beach and on the next holiday I asked him how it went. He said, 'It was absolutely great, it went down a storm and I don't think people realised that it had been written for me.' I do hope I haven't let the cat out of the bag.

Our French friends with Martin and Jack on Mummie's lap

More friends in Benidorm
Anne and David with Terry and Anne

Four young lads owned and worked in the café shop where Peggy and I used to have our eleven o'clock coffee. They were extremely nice people to us and we were always in conversation about something or another. I seem to remember that one of them was a Real Madrid supporter and one of them was Barcelona, and they were always interested in English football. The conversation more often than not turned to talking about last night's game. I can only say that one of the nicest things about going to Benidorm was the friends that we made. There were so many of them, and what I would like to do is to go back, but I can't. My mind is such at the moment that I cannot go anywhere where Peggy and I went and enjoyed ourselves together. One of these days, maybe, who knows?

Anne and Martin and Melissa and Jack came to Benidorm fairly regularly during our October break and they liked it very much. Jack in particular liked the water, he kept his grandfather going all day with either swimming or playing football or running or jumping. Martin liked the French people because he could speak fluent French and that meant that he and Roger and Anne-Marie got on well. It helped us because although Roger was very good with English we sometimes had to have a translation of what they said.

We continued to go to Spain on that regular basis right up until the last few days of Mummie's life. She used to say to me, 'Well, you're the one who has to do all the work.' However we used to get there, we used to relax, we would meet our friends and we were in the sunshine, there was very little else that we really wanted. I can tell you the number of times that we sat with the windows wide open on the balcony, looking out over the promenade and the sea, and said to ourselves how lucky we were that we were still able to be like this with each other. We were lucky that we were able to do what we could do and more than that, we were lucky that we were still in love with each other which we were when we were married. It always ended up in a cuddle and you can imagine just how we felt.

18

On Mummie's eightieth birthday we thought it would be a good idea if we invited my two brothers, my sister and some of the other relatives that we hadn't seen for years and years because of what had gone on in the past. So we sent out invitations to quite a lot of people who hadn't actually been to our birthdays and other celebrations for many years. We were extremely grateful when they replied that they would be there, particularly Brian and Bob and Doreen and Arthur and Jean and Marge. It was extremely nice to see them and I was pleased to think that from that moment onwards, right up until today, we have been on very fond terms. We have visited each other's houses, I've visited a few days on holiday on a number of occasions with both Brian and Bob and I've looked forward to them immensely. I'm just happy that in the end we were able to meet up with each other and enjoy each other's company. I'm sure that that will continue now for some time to come.

The party, as well as you can imagine, was another Skelton party where nothing stands still for more than a few seconds, with plenty of food, drink and activity. Another young lady who came was Maureen, the hairdresser in Elizabeth house. She was the hairdresser when Elizabeth House opened in March 1987, and she did Peggy's hair every week or every time she needed it done. I also had my hair cut by Maureen and so we came to know her well. She knew a lot about our family and we knew a lot about hers, and that connection has continued because I still go and have my hair cut by Maureen. Her attitude towards me has been extremely sympathetic and she understood how difficult it would be for me to recover from the loss of somebody like Peggy, who everyone loved and everyone got on so well with. As I have said before Peggy was just a very special person.

The main feature of this eightieth birthday party was the fact that on the same day, 14th May, it was Gemma's twenty-first birthday and two weeks earlier it had been Joanna's twenty-first birthday. You can see from the photograph that we were celebrating all these birthdays. A strange thing with regard to Gemma and Joanna is that they are now in their thirties and recently they have both had baby boys – Oliver James for Joanna and Henry John for Gemma, two weeks apart in their birth. It's likely they will become just as good friends as Gemma and Joanna have been over the years. Life is full of bizarre twists and I am sure there are many more of those twists still to come.

At this time Bobby and Rachael were becoming very close to each other and it was obvious that they were extremely happy together. Rachael, a lovely girl, fitted into the family very well and she pointed Bobby in the right direction. It was something that he needed and she was the right girl to do it. Rachael came to us after she had been going out with Bobby for some time and wedding plans were in the air, and she asked us if we would adopt her as another grandchild. As far as I can remember she didn't have any grand-parents, with the exception of a grandfather who was in Canada and she had never heard from him, and she wanted to be our grandchild as opposed to a grand-daughter in law. We readily agreed to adopt as she is a lovely girl who fits into the family easily.

Joanna was a very talented artist, she is a doctor now. She has done some really magnificent work which of course hangs in her parents' home, but she copied a photograph of Mummie and me, a picture of some function that we were at and obviously smiling away. I can tell you that it catches the eye of many people when they come into the living room at Elizabeth House.

My son Martin said to me that my book would not be complete without mentioning the Skelton ancestry. I thought he was quite right and so I will tell you a little about the Skeltons in Scotland and the trip that Martin and Anne, Mummie and I made in August 2002. Lesley and Clive subsequently caught up with us while we were in Kinross. Martin had spent a great deal of time, money and patience over a very long period in the whole research of the Skeltons in the eighteenth and nineteenth centuries. He came to the conclusion that all the Skeltons in the family tree at some time in their lives lived in either Orwell or Kinross. Now he has written a six page document which shows that the Skeltons were formidable people in that particular part of Scotland: writers, sheriffs, MP, Secretary of State, inn-owners and stage coach proprietors. There is a private Skelton cemetery. We went to a cemetery in Kinross, trying to find a particular person, and we came across some people who knew where this particular Skelton's grave was. They were flabbergasted when they realised that they were talking to Skeltons and said that we were indeed a formidable family in Kinross, and that there was a book at the local library with a large section devoted to the Skelton dynasty. We felt we were somewhat famous.

In Martin's document it says, 'The Rudiment weekly magazine of 1772 says none is more famous in Scotland for skill in cookery than Mrs Skelton of Kinross Green Hill.'

One of the Skelton's homes

The Skelton private burial ground

Our Scottish transport

If anyone is interested in this document that Martin has prepared, and I can tell you that it has a great many names and a great deal of information that people might like to read, I'd only be too pleased to send you a copy in order that you can understand a little more of the ancestry of the Skelton family.

19

Coming up to our sixtieth wedding anniversary, Mummie's arthritis was getting worse. She didn't complain too much about it but there were times when she would say to me, 'You know every bone in my body aches.' It started to actually make her feel somewhat uncomfortable when she couldn't do the jobs that she would normally take on. But she wasn't a complainer and she never lost that laughter in her eyes and her smile, she was just one of those people who was just determined to make the most of life. For our sixtieth wedding anniversary, of course we had the usual card from the Queen and a party was arranged by our children, in Portsmouth. The dress for people who were coming was to be what people would be wearing in 1944 and as you will see there were different styles – some were nurses, there was an ARP warden, some were from the navy and I myself was dressed in a naval uniform. I didn't know what I was going to be until I arrived. I had a naval uniform and Mummie had a head-dress, the type of head-dress that she would have worn when we married on 2nd November 1944.

Martin took charge of the proceedings and he came as Captain Shady Lane who was captain of HMS *Guardian*. I've told you one or two stories about Shady Lane and Martin continued along that line when he was giving his speech. Jackie gave a speech in support of her mum and dad and I must say for someone who's not normally known for speech writing, she did a really, very good job of presenting the speech and thanking us for what we had done for the children. Then it came to my turn to make a speech and say a very big thank you for the support that our family had given not only to us but to each other in good times and bad. It was another one of those parties, and a highlight which is still talked about was Jamie who came without his fancy dress on and then changed into the pukka chicken. The pukka chicken was the sort of thing the family used to do at parties and Jamie had the idea of not only doing the pukka chicken dance but also dressing up as a chicken, and I have to say it was well done Jamie.

Melissa herself had a great deal to do with the organisation, she put her mum and dad absolutely straight on what was required on a sixtieth wedding anniversary. She was kind enough to get a large photograph of Mummie and me on our wedding day and got the grandchildren all to sign it; this hangs in the living room at Elizabeth House. She also had a collection for Mummie to go on a boat trip that she'd always talked about from Benidorm. Rachael had 30 bona fide first class stamps printed which you can see from the photograph. Wonderful idea!

The family

Simply still very much in love

Jamie and Pukka Chicken

In 2004 I was asked to do one more game show in Elizabeth House. I thought about it for some time. The problem was the pianist. Peggy had then not played the piano for twelve months because of the arthritis in her fingers and so whether it was going to go on or not had to be in her hands, as it were. She decided to start and practise just to see how well she could do it, how good she could get and after a time, a matter of weeks or so, she

179

decided that perhaps she would be able to play. She wouldn't only be doing her own two pieces, but of course she had to accompany some of the singers and their songs. However that's what we did, we put it on and Martin generously came up from Portsmouth and filmed a video of the show. We have recently turned it into a DVD. Mummie did her two pieces, her two Chopin waltzes and all I can tell you is that she played them absolutely brilliantly, it was a superb performance by her and the applause at the end shows just how pleased people were with her playing. It is now one of the DVDs that I play on a very regular basis because it shows just how much we enjoyed each other's company, as we performed a couple of songs together. The main attraction to me is that I see her playing; it's as if she's in the room with me. I mostly have a little cry but that doesn't stop me watching it. When I see her playing the piano and smiling and laughing with other people, that's how she was and that's how she'll stay in my memory forever.

Another thing which used to happen was that I used to sing to her. I know that might sound strange to some people but very often she would say to me, 'Oh, you haven't sung to me lately', and so I would sing to her some of the songs that we associated with each other. You know the sort of songs 'I'll be your sweetheart if you will be mine', 'I'll see you in apple blossom time', all those sorts of songs which we held very dearly as something which had brought us together. She used to like 'You are my sunshine' and 'Let me tell you sweetest I'm in love with you' and there were times she would say, 'Well, you haven't put your hat on have you?' because I always used to sing in a bow tie and a hat. So I had to put the hat on and when we were finished joining in together she used to say, 'Now give me a cuddle and take me to bed.' I heard that many times.

By now I am afraid that the arthritis was getting worse, a great deal worse, and Peggy was a regular visitor to the surgery. We had a wonderful doctor in Dr Dyson and Mummie said she felt so much better after she'd been to see her because she was a great comfort and knew what to say to patients who were struggling. The receptionists at Lincoln House were very good, particularly Julie with whom we always had a laugh. She knew we went on holidays many times and she was always wanting to come with us; I used to say, 'Well just arrive at the airport with your suitcase and you can come,' but she never did. We had some great fun together talking about our holidays and I'm sure it took away the pain that Mummie was having at that time. She was using a stick all the time now and in fact there were times when she used a wheelchair, not all the time, there were certain times when the pain was bearable enough to just walk. She wasn't the sort of person to complain about it, although you could sometimes see the pain in her eyes enough to tell you she wasn't having a great time. It did not stop us going away, we continued to go for three months in Benidorm and we enjoyed every moment of that.

Unfortunately I now have to record the death of Ann, Martin's wife, a wonderful person. She was loved by everybody, she was fun, and she was generous to the extreme. She loved her family, her two children – you could not say anything against either Melissa or Warren while in Ann's hearing. She was a person we got to like very much and her death was a tragedy. Her father had died of an aneurism of the aorta. When Ann became unwell she went to see a doctor who knew her quite well and he thought she had a minor stroke. Martin then took Ann to the hospital where she saw a young Australian doctor. Martin told the story of the history of Ann's father, and they knew the facts and the details, but the doctor decided that it was minor stroke and sent Ann home. Unfortunately she was only home a couple of days and then she died, of a similar condition to her father's. I can't tell you just how deeply upset the whole family were; it was a tragedy in every sense of the word. She loved Mummie and Mummie loved her; Ann treated Mummie as if she was her second mother.

Martin complained, the NHS Trust was involved, solicitors were involved and the Trust sat by their version that everything was done that could have been done. It went on and on. In the end the verdict was that if Ann had been kept in that night she would have been saved and so the Trust settled out of court with a substantial sum of money to Martin for the loss of his wife. Of course money was not the object at all, it was pure and simply to make certain they would be more careful in future.

The deterioration in Mummie's arthritis was quite quick really, you could see a difference every month or so. It wasn't long before the wheelchair was used more often and it wasn't long before she was in it every time we were going out anywhere. It was particularly useful in Benidorm on the long straight promenade – we could sit there and there was no problem and as I had the car it was possible to transport the wheelchair around. Along with that was the fact that Mummie wasn't able to do things that normal people could do. She couldn't lift her arms up to comb her hair and so I had to put a parting in her hair. I didn't get it in the right place many times but I did my best. Then I had to shower her and when I was drying her down with a towel I had to make sure I did not rub her too hard because it hurt her bones. She did not complain as such, but she let me know if I was in any way trying to dry her too hard using too hard a movement. Then when I was putting her socks on I had to make sure her heel went into the heel of the sock. I had a little difficulty with that particular job, and with tying her shoe laces where I either tied them too tight or too loose. We made fun of everything that I had to do. For me it was simply carrying on with our love match.

In Benidorm we were on the third floor, and of course I had to get her out of the apartment in the wheelchair. I had to carry the beach bag, a chair I was going to use, a windbreak, a mallet and also a sun umbrella. I had to get all that into the lift from the third floor down and then get it out of the lift, and then get it to the front gate. I had to try and unlock the gate with all this gear on and get Mummie out. Fortunately we only had to walk across the road to the promenade and down a wooden slipway, very handy for the wheelchair. Then I had to get her on to the beach. The first job was to throw the gear I had on my back on to the sand, and then I put up my chair and got her up and sitting on my chair. Then I got her wheelchair off the walkway on to the sand and got her settled in to the wheelchair. Then a decision had to be made whether to put the umbrella up or have the windbreak up, depending on just how warm the sunshine was. Then she might say to me, 'I think I will have my cardigan on,' so I would put it on her. Her comment then was often, 'John, you have creased this cardigan up.' I can tell you it didn't quite cause a smile. There you are, that was the sort of things that had to be done.

Fortunately because we were right next to the walkway everyone spoke to her. Even if they did not know her people would come over to speak to her, she was a chatty person and she could talk for a long time. We always had some help. I remember for two or three years there were four Dutch teachers who used to go there in June and sit fairly close to where we used to park ourselves. They used to come over to talk. The two men knew we left the beach around five o'clock and they used to come over and help me get everything together and push her up the walkway and up to the apartment. They were lovely people, I wish I could recall their names.

We still kept up the process of going to Benidorm three times a year and we still met many of our friends. Anne and David helped us a tremendous amount – they used to meet us at the apartment gates and help us to get up to our room and on our journey back they always came to see us into the taxi to take us back to the airport. Anne used to arrive with a present for Mummie of twenty-eight meringues – she knew that Mummie had a sweet tooth and this meant she could have one a day during our stay there.

There were two other people that we met up with again during the period of Peggy not being able to get around very well. One was Aunt Ciss, the lady I met on the doorstep when I arrived home from Iceland and we were about to get married. She was living with Peggy's mother at the time and was Peggy's father's sister. Through Martin's research, not only of the Skelton ancestry but of the Goater ancestry as well, we came across Aunt Ciss and we met her again and had a very nice time with her and her family. We also met, once again through Martin's efforts on the computer, Peter and Diana Goater. Peter was Peggy's cousin, he had come to our wedding and we had not met or been in touch with each other for years. Martin found them and he took us to see them and their lovely family. We have kept in touch with them ever since. It was surprising the talk that went on between Aunt Ciss and her family and us, and again with Peter and Diane – they were able to talk to Peggy about old times. I know that Mummie was extremely pleased that she had met these people whom she had not been in touch with for many, many years.

Over the years a number of the grandchildren have got married. Melissa with Darren, Warren and Vicky, Bobbie and Rachael, Sophie and Doug, and I am pleased to say that as I write this there may be another wedding going to take place as Jessica and Jamie have now fixed the date for their wedding. I have said previously that this is not a book purely and simply about the Skelton family – it is a book about Mummie and me, our life together. I have tried to make it a love story because that is exactly what our life together had always been – a story of two people who fell in love and were in love with each other from day one to the end.

20

Our sixty-fifth wedding anniversary was coming up. We decided at this time it would just be a family affair and that is what happened. The one special part of the occasion was that Mummie made her first and only speech. She only said a few words, but I can tell you that those few words overshadowed everything else that happened on that particular day. She was becoming frail and these sorts of things were an ordeal for her, but being the person that she was she stood up for it and gave a speech. It was not expected and those people who heard it were impressed and touched.

The picture says it all

I'm afraid Mummie was now in a position where she was able to do very little for herself. In fact it was really a 24 hours a day job looking after her. I won't go into detail but I can tell you there were days when I felt absolutely exhausted. However we went out every day; she would be wrapped up in her blanket, gloves and scarves and anything that would keep her warm. She was still chatty and talking to people, and people were very kind to her in as much there was always a few words to be exchanged. We used to go to the newsagents every day to get our newspapers and the people in there who ran the shop, Kieran and his sister who I always called Sis because that is what he used to call her, they were very nice to Mummie. She was unable to get into the shop, but Kieran used to go out and chat away with her and she was extremely pleased to have somebody to chat to while I was in the shop. At the weekends Sis's two daughters were there, twins they were, you certainly could not tell the difference between them, one named Rita and the other one Unurvashi. Two lovely girls who knew our family because we were always chatting to each other. They also had a brother who wasn't in there very often but he was the complete opposite in size – they were small and petite and he was something like six feet five. Peggy used to complain sometimes I was in there too long, she used to send Kieran back in there to say, 'Come on John, Peggy's getting cold out there.' I still go in there and I still chat away to them. A lovely family and I shall always remember their kindness to me after Peggy's death.

Of course when we were in the house Peggy was able to do very little, but the one job she continued to do was to wash up because she said I never did it well enough. She used to shuffle to the kitchen and do the dishes. I am

Not another story!

186

sure she was quite right, I most probably didn't do it to a very high standard, but other than that I did almost everything else. Getting her up at night to use her commode, I used to have to get her up off the bed and get her on to the commode and then get her back into bed. She had very strong painkillers and a morphine patch, which I used to apply and I had to make certain she didn't take more painkillers than she should. The days went by and people came in to see her and we went out every day, so she was not in any way, from the outside anyway, what one would call an unhappy person.

It was two o'clock in the morning, and I had to call an ambulance for Mummie. I could see she was not very well and she was taken to hospital. Unfortunately things started to go wrong and she was taken to intensive care. I had to get in touch with the children and they had to make their way to the hospital, and then while she was in intensive care she was seen by a specialist. By then Jackie had arrived and she was with me, and together we heard from the specialist that Mummie was in a serious condition. I said 'What do you mean? Has she a few months or a few weeks?' He said 'No, I am afraid I am talking about a very few hours.' Jackie and I fell into each other's arms and simply cried.

What was going through my mind all the time, were the last words that she said before she went into intensive care: 'I do feel bad John, please help me.' Then she said, 'I am sorry to have been such a burden to you – you have been so kind.' Although those were her last words, her eyes were saying just how desperate she felt. Sadness is not a big enough word.

What the specialist told us was that probably the previous day her bowel had burst and so it was slowly poisoning her. There was very little they could do so she was taken into a ward on her own and we were there. The one redeeming feature, I suppose, was that Roland was there holding her hand. The nurses told us that although she wouldn't be able to speak or anything like that, she knew exactly what was going on and those of us who were present – Martin, Roland, Jackie and John, Jamie and of course myself. We just talked to her and the nurses assured us that she could hear us. At the very end Roland was holding her hand, the tears were rolling down his face, and I could see from the look in Mummie's eyes that a reconciliation had taken place in the last few seconds of her life.

The reconciliation was over an incident some years previously when Roland held his sixtieth birthday party, and Mummie and I found ourselves at the bottom end of two separate tables while the top table was for the president of the golf club. She was extremely upset about that and when the meal was over we had to leave with Jackie and John. It was a very long time before she ever really got over it, but at the end of her life I could see by the way she was looking at him that a reconciliation had taken place, I am certain of that.

From the moment that Mummie left us, my thoughts were that it takes two to tango. When there is only one person left the rhythm of life has gone and the one left behind becomes a different person. I knew that from day one the old John Skelton had really died and the new one was never going to be the same person again. I knew it, and it is as true today as it was then. No matter what the experts say, that time is the great healer, to me that is not the case. Time is just a means of getting through one day at a time and having the strength to struggle to survive.

What happened from that moment onwards is very hazy for me. I really was totally useless and paralysed. The children were there and of course Lesley came down from Blackpool and Martin had to take charge of what was going to happen next, such as the funeral arrangements. It was going to be held from Jackie's house in St. Albans, so she was heavily involved as well. I wanted to go back and see Mummie in the funeral parlour – Matthew and Lesley came with me. She looked beautiful, no longer in any pain, her long, slender piano-player's fingers were entwined and she looked very peaceful. All I wanted to do was to cuddle her. I knew that was not possible and I am not sure if I just kissed her forehead, I don't really remember exactly what I was doing at that time. I know it was sad. When I think about it now it is sad, but I am glad I went and saw her in the parlour because she certainly did look absolutely pain free and that was something which hadn't happened for a very long time.

I know what went through my mind quite often were the stock phrases that she used to use. When people would say, 'Aren't you worried?' she would say, 'No I don't have to worry because John will know what to do, he will sort it out.' Well he couldn't this time, and someone else had done the sorting. I had very many cards from people, including one from an old friend of my sister's, Emmie. She wrote what Peggy had written to her in a letter quite recently: 'John was a wonderful person and a wonderful husband and he was always the same from the time he got up in the morning until he went to bed at night. He made my life really worth living and I never want to be without him.' I thought well, that was us, we just lived for each other.

It took me back just a little when I found an old diary that Peggy had kept – the date on it was 22nd or 23rd March 1935. In it she said, 'I am now the leader of the cheery chatterers and have been for about four months.' The cheery chatterers were just two people, her and her friend, and the object was to go along and knock at old people's doors and try to cheer them up.

What she did tell me later of course was that her mother would only let her go to those old people who were members of the church. We did often talk about the cheery chatterers – she was quite proud of the fact she was the leader. She lived the whole of her life that way – her task was to make people as happy as she was herself.

I recall one rather spooky thing – when Martin and I and Jackie were registering Mummie's death, we got to her name and called her Evelyn Peggy, but from that moment onwards the registrar referred to her as Peggy. We questioned her and said, 'Why would you call her Peggy?' and she said, 'I just thought that she would like it, it came to my mind that she would like the name of Peggy.' We told her, 'Yes you are quite right she has always been called Peggy or Mummie, but never Evelyn.'

On the 28th of each month I light a candle at 11.45, which was the time of her death, and I drink a little toast not only to Mummie but to Ann as well. On two separate occasions the match I have used to light the candle has got stuck in the candle itself and then there have been two flames, and those flames have kept going through the whole of the quarter of an hour which I normally have the candle alight for. Who knows, it is up to people to make up their minds about these sorts of things, but they did happen.

Of course the funeral came; it was on the 12th of October. All I can say is there were numerous friends and neighbours, and a very large family gathering. I would not want to name any particular person because they were all there to pay their last respects to someone I know they all loved. The day came and the day went, and for many days after then and right up until this moment the phrase she said goes through my mind time after time: 'You will never forget me John will you?' 'Of course I won't,' I said, and that is the case. Of course I won't and I never will. She knew that I meant every word of my reply.

Some years previously Lesley had moved to Blackpool and Mummie and I had been there on one or two occasions. I still make the journey up to Blackpool to see Lesley. The one big factor for me is that Cleveleys, which is next door to Blackpool, is where we had our honeymoon way back in 1944 and walking along the north pier and dancing in the tower ballroom was part and parcel of our honeymoon. Now came the chance for us to try and find exactly the house that we stayed in. We had stayed in a house that belonged to Peggy's uncle. He had been evacuated there during the war through the Ministry of Pensions and he stayed with Peggy's mother and we went up and stayed in his house. The problem was that he was a top civil servant and his address was a secret. All I can remember about it is that it was a long road and it led right on to the promenade and to the tracks for the tram and we used to make that journey into Blackpool itself from Cleveleys. We tried many times and through various channels to try and find this house, I have failed so far but I keep on trying. There is one family, the Johnsons, and one time I knocked at Julie Johnson's door and told her the story and she did her best with her four lovely daughters to help to find this address. I am sure that we have come close and I am quite certain that having met Julie's family and her father that she has done her best to try to find the address that we stayed in. I know the road and I know the sort of whereabouts but I can't establish the actual house. I haven't heard from Julie for some time but when I go to Blackpool I have always called and met her and we've talked about this honeymoon address. I hope I find it sometime but I think now it is a long time ago and people's memories are really quite short.

I made myself a strategy, if I were to survive this particular critical time for me. I decided that I had to go out each day, which I still do. I go out each day with one or two jobs in mind which have to be done. I also take my friend George to do his shopping on a Tuesday and I take him to get his pension on a Thursday, and I also do one or two other little jobs for him. I get his paper every day. There are other jobs which I still do and that keeps me occupied during the morning. I have already talked about the people in the newsagents who I talk to on a regular basis, and I have to tell you about Santander too because I go in there quite a few times each week. Sometimes I just sit on their couch and I talk to people who come and sit beside me, but on the main I go in because they have been very friendly towards me. One particular young lady, Emma Hayes, used to quite often come and speak to me, she took an interest in an old person who was in a state of bereavement. It was nice that someone like her should take an interest in someone who was in his ninetieth year, and I wrote to the manager of the bank and told him so. Her colleague Christine was also very nice and chatty to me and both of them, Emma and Christine, showed a great deal of interest in the book. I would just like to say that people such as Emma and Christine help me to get through very difficult days.

I normally arrive back home by about twelve or twelve thirty. I have my lunch to prepare and then I have to set about various jobs that need to be done in the house, washing and cleaning and all those sort of things, which help to pass away the afternoon. Jackie's John rings me every afternoon just to have a little chat about how things are going and I really look forward to and appreciate that call. I then watch 'Deal or No Deal', it's my favourite TV programme, in fact I tell people it's my fix because I do not watch any other programmes. My interest in everything has gone, whether it be football or politics, what is going on in the world or newspapers, news bulletins, I simply can't watch them and have no time for them. I certainly watch the family DVDs very often and listen to Mummie playing the piano. I watch them after I have cooked my meal and I always drink a little whiskey. I am always in bed by something like six thirty or seven o'clock, I get into bed, I am nice and warm, and I just say to myself, 'Well I have survived another day.'

I have kept Mummie's ashes in the bedroom. I have done this because she used to say she didn't want her ashes to be put out in the cold, out in the ground all on her own, getting wet. She hated the cold, she hated getting wet, and she was frightened of the dark. I told her that I would keep them and that is what I have done – her ashes are in the bedroom with the clothes that she wore the day before she died. I have spoken to Martin about what to do with my ashes. They will be mixed with Mummie's ashes and we will be together again.

21

Life goes on. I used to go to visit Brian and Jean, certainly once or maybe twice a year. Martin was kind enough to pick me up, and on the way we would call in and see Peter and Diana Goater and then go on to see Brian and Jean. They lived fairly close to Felixstowe and on the itinerary would always be a visit to Felixstowe to the school that I went to, to the house that I was born in, the house that I lived in, the railway station that I lived next to, and the promenade and the boating lake. It was all a journey of nostalgia and I have kept that contact up. I also go to see Bobby in Cornwall, where they had four years being evacuated in the war, and then Bobby for a very long time felt that the only place he wanted to retire to was Cornwall. I think he was around sixty when he retired and I will include a photograph of the bungalow that he and his wife Marge built on their own, living in a caravan on that site at the age of sixty. I might tell you that it is the second home that he has built, but to achieve this at the age of sixty, I think they both need congratulating.

Marge and Bob's bungalow

In 1945 Mummie and I had a holiday in Penryn, and we went and spent a week in the same house that Bobby and Brian were evacuated to. To us they were Mr and Mrs Lilly, but to Brian they were Aunt and Uncle. There was no running water, no electricity, no light and the toilet was at the bottom of the garden. Mr and Mrs Lilly were very good to us, very nice people. They had been devastated when their two boys Brian and Bobby left after four years and they talked of very little else.

For a long time before Mummie died we used to go and see Doreen and Arthur on a fairly regular basis. They lived close by and it was no distance in the car to go and see them. I think mentioned that during my heart operation Mummie actually lived with Doreen and Arthur while I was in the hospital.

Some three or four years ago Gemma, Jackie's daughter, moved to New Zealand. She was only going to stay a year but she has been there ever since. She went with her boyfriend who was a Kiwi, he had been living in England for about twelve years. Now this brought up the whole story of my mother's sister Gladys, who emigrated to New Zealand, followed her boyfriend and married out there, and lived out there for eight years, had five children and sadly committed suicide. That story came back to life with Gemma being in New Zealand. You see nothing was ever spoken in our family about Gladys from the moment that they received the information of her death. My mother never spoke about it, nor did my grandfather, my grandmother, no one ever spoke about it at all. So when Gemma went to New Zealand it

The picture that started the whole New Zealand story. Gladys Collins with her three children and Reg Collins

194

The New Zealand relatives

sprang to my mind that perhaps we were going to be able to find a trail of Gladys Wood and the five children. We didn't know her married name, but using the fact that she had actually emigrated following her boyfriend and his family we found that his name was Reg Collins. Eventually my sister's son Alan's wife Janet found a photograph in an old box, I'm sure it came from my mother, down to my sister. The photograph kicked everything off and when it was sent to New Zealand, it stirred the memories of many people. E-mails were flying backwards and forwards, and in the end Martin and Gemma found twenty-two new relatives. Both Martin and Gemma did a tremendous amount of work with e-mails etc., in trying to find the relatives and of course had great success.

The relatives knew very little about the story, in fact some of them had hardly seen each other for some time. Some had been told that Gladys fell from the bridge, but that wasn't the case because we have copies of the 1933 local paper with the story and then the coroner's report, saying that she had committed suicide. Gemma, by constant looking and e-mailing, had found the relatives and she had got them together to begin with and then Jackie, my daughter, and I decided that we would go to New Zealand and that is what we did. We went out there, we went to Gemma's house and we met these people. The story made the front pages of the local paper in Auckland, and it also made the front pages of the local paper in Hemel Hempstead.

195

New Zealand – April 2012

Wednesday 18th

I left Elizabeth House at 5 o'clock pm and made my way to Heathrow for the 10 o'clock pm flight to Singapore. John and Jackie drove me to the Airport and of course Jackie came with me to New Zealand. John came into the Airport and we had coffee etc and the he said 'Goodbye' The 10 o'clock came and we took off very smoothly in an Airbus, very comfortable seats for the 12 and a half hour flight. The cabin crew were excellent and we had some very good food. After dinner I took 2 sleeping tablets and then spent the next 5 or 6 hours sleeping. We arrived at around 6.30 where we had a room booked for the night in an Airport Hotel. Fell into bed and had a good night's sleep.

Thursday 19th

Out of bed at 5.30, had wheelchair service to check in etc for the next flight which was at 8.45am and was a 10 hour flight. Still good service, nice seats and excellent food. Had a couple of hours sleep and arrived in Auckland at 12 o'clock midnight. Was met by Steve and Gemma and had a really lovely warm welcoming feeling. Had a drink or two and in bed by 3 o'clock.

Saturday 21st

Because of time change etc we are now into Saturday, everything is going to plan. Got up at 9 o'clock feeling very relaxed. Have been out all day, weather was excellent, spent some time with Gemma and Steve and also Jackie of course and we went to North Head also to see one of Devonport's Volcanoes. Walked through caves which had been built to hold guns etc in the 1800s to hold off any attacks which at that time would have come from Russia. Had our picnic lunch overlooking Cheltenham Beach and Rangitoto Volcano. Had coffee in Devonport Village and then had a conversation with a nice lady in the Tourist Office who I told the reason why we were in New Zealand. She was a good listener. Have now settled tomorrow's plans.

Sunday 22nd

It is the day of my 88th birthday. The sun is shining and I am quite excited. A surprise package had been set up and I now just had to wait and see what was in store. I had a little cry with Mummy and then opened my cards, I had to be ready by 11.30 and we set off to Auckland. The Sky Towers which is the tallest building in the Southern Hemisphere was the destination. What a fantastic building. We sat and had a drink looking out over a fantastic view of Auckland and through the harbour out to sea. Watched people have a Bungy Jump. Unfortunately they were fully booked and so I had to be content with watching!!!!

We then went to the revolving restaurant for a meal and so as we were eating we enjoyed the scenery of the whole city. The food was excellent and there was more to come as a birthday cake was the produced. What a surprise, a few tears and then we enjoyed the cake. We then went to the Casino for a little gamble, Steve winning around 100 dollars and I lost about 20. What a fantastic day full of surprises. We came back to the house, had a few drinks and played Upword, had a cheese supper and then went to bed. My thanks to Gemma and Steve for organising such a wonderful day, never to be forgotten.

Monday 23rd

Woke up to a very warm sunny day. The day that the reporter from the local newspaper came to hear about our story of my Aunt Gladys who came to New Zealand in 1924 and the fact that we were not only here to see Gemma and Steve but to meet our relatives from New Zealand who we have only recently discovered. The reporter was very interested in the whole story.

We spent the rest of the morning in the garden reading, sun tan lotion for protection. We had our lunch in the garden. Set off to the ferry which takes us from Devonport to Auckland Harbour. We walked along the sea front which was full of tourists and sea front cafes. The boats in the middle of the harbour were magnificent, costing millions of pound each. We made up our mind which ones we would purchase. Our destination was the Fish Market to buy fish in particular Whelks. First failure of the holiday. No Whelks!! It was a good job we had stopped and had a drink at one of the cafes as we were able to joke about the failure without upsetting the hosts.

We caught the ferry back and called into a small bay and watched Steve have a swim. His hand strokes in the waves were not bad but he must practice more. Back home to a really nice fish dinner which Steve cooked. The dinner took a little more time than expected. Jackie had 3 large glasses of wine before dinner, just about finished her dinner before collapsing on the sofa – fell asleep. Another great day, bring on tomorrow.

Tuesday 24th

Another day . More sunshine and I was told to be ready for 11:30 am and we were having a day out on the West Coast. The place was Piha, a one hour drive from Devonport. A real beauty spot. Sandy bay surrounded by a rugged coast line, with very few people on the sand. It is a bay well known by surfers with strong tidal currents. Swimmers take care. Steven had his usual swim, I had a paddle. Jackie laid on a towel flat out. Temp was 23 degrees. On the way to Piha we stopped for coffee and I had a long chat with the lady who ran the little Post Office, open four days a week, 2 hours each day. After our conversation we knew a great deal about each other. She told me her only skill was to chatter ! We spent several hours on the beach, had a lovely lunch and Steven pulled from the lunch basket a bottle of ice cold beer. The man's a genius ! Back to Devonport and pre dinner drinks – mine being beer and whisky. Had a really nice Sweet and Sour Chicken. Played cards, watched Deal or No Deal and then to bed . Exhausted !! The whole day was awesome !! (I was told this was a well known N.Z. expression).

Wednesday 25th

The day nearly started with a disaster. We were told to be ready for 6 o'clock morning time as it was ANZAC Day, a day similar to our Remembrance Day. Fortunately Jackie read an evening paper which told us that the ceremony did not start until 10 o'clock. Disaster averted! The whole ceremony – the march past, the service etc – was very moving. Everyone was given an ANZAC DAY COMMEMORATION programme. I sang with gusto particularly when it came to God Save The Queen. There were a few thousand people attending and in the sunshine the parade etc was spectacular.

We came home , sat in a lovely warm garden, had our lunch and then made our way to the garden centre. Returned home for our pre-dinner drinks. Chilli with chicken plus couscous, delicious. Never have I been so adventurous.. Played our usual cards, watched Deal or No Deal and then to bed. What more can anyone ask from a New .Zealand adventure.

Thursday 26th

Today was going to be a long day. Steve was driving us some 300 miles which takes in the area where Gladys Wood and Reg Collins lived when arriving in New Zealand. We stopped on the way at a cheese making plant and had a very nice lunch and then drove through some beautiful countryside in the sunshine. It reminded me of the Lake District.

First stop was the small town of Putaruru which is where Reg Collins' mother and father had their bakery and confectionary shop. We got some info from the tourist department and then the local library and from that information and speaking to some other people we came to the conclusion that, although there was not a bakery shop now, the shop would have been one of a little collection of shops called the High Street. A passer by told us that in the 1920s this area would have been a poor run down area. No wonder Gladys was not very happy.

We then went to the cemetery where Gladys Wood or Collins as she would have been known was buried. Had difficulty finding the spot. Steven phones the Council who told us the spot and that in fact when she was buried there was a head stone. The lady was going to send a photo of the head stones. It has not arrived yet. We then went to the bridge that Gladys jumped to her death. Extremely moving standing on the spot where the disaster happened.

We made our way back having left at 9.30 am we arrived back at 6.30pm. My only disappointment was that we had driven some 300 miles and I only saw 6 sheep. Obviously not the land of sheep.

Friday 27th

A new day and a new adventure. We were going to Kelly Tarltons which is an aquarium where people can swim in a cage with sharks, very large sting rays and all types of fish. It had other attractions such as a mock up of Captain Scott and Shackleton's expedition, also a journey through the Antarctic where we came across some 40 – 50 penguins. The whole experience took several hours. I need not mention that I was the only one who did not swim with the sharks.

Returned home, had our pre-dinner drinks, played our usual cards of which I am sad to say at the moment I am bottom of the pile – due to receiving bad cards and I suspect conspiracy !

Saturday 28th

The day I have waited a very long time for had actually arrived. Great excitement. Of course there was a lot of preparation to do. The food had been purchased yesterday but then had to be prepared. The house had to look in pristine condition and so there was a great deal of action. I had my speech to prepare and so was excluded from the morning hurly burly.

2 o'clock was kick off time, we were already looking out of the front window when the first visitors arrived around 2.15 pm. I thought that they would arrive as strangers and leave as new found friends and relatives but I was wrong. From their very first arrival they were warm, sincere and as excited as we were to meet each other. There were many cards and presents and there was no time for a warm up period, straight away everyone was in conversation with details of the family's past, photos and documents being exchanged. Everyone had a different version of the same subject. Even teenage children were interested in what happened in the past.

I thanked Martin for his tremendous effort, Gemma for her constant research and Desiree who was the main New Zealand contact. Of course I told the story when the fateful letter arrived to tell of the suicide of Gladys. It was because of her desperate home sickness which drove her to leave behind her husband and five children. I was asked afterwards to make a copy of the speech and send it back to New Zealand. Gemma then led them all singing Happy Birthday.

It is very difficult for me to describe the atmosphere of the whole afternoon. It was compassionate, sincere and everyone trying to piece together the past. A positive triumph for the effort of Gemma and Steve in organising the party. When everyone left they left with a warm appreciation and a farewell with the words we must meet again and soon.

We finished with our usual game of cards where Steve and I remained sober but two young ladies drank as much wine as possible, Gemma ending up in the garden stuck in the middle of a rose bush. I went to bed 10 o'clock. Exhausted. Tomorrow is a day to chill out

Sunday 29th

Exhausted and tired but we were all very proud of ourselves for the way the whole day had played out. Energy was very low, we just drove to Mt. Victoria and admired the wonderful view over Auckland the sea and harbour. The weather was fine but little sunshine. We returned via a very unusual French coffee shop for refreshment. We had our lunch at home then Jackie, Steve and I set about working in the garden. Jackie planting her herb garden, Steve doing the heavy work where as I first pruned the roses and then supervised!

We had our usual drinks and surprise, surprise I was told we were having a Hot Bombay Curry for dinner. After I fainted I agreed to try this new experience and I enjoyed it, I enjoyed it very much. We played our usual card game. My luck had changed I won 3 games. Am now in the running to be the champ. In bed 9 o'clock – Goodnight

Monday 30th

Today I was told to be ready for 11o'clock. We were going to a museum in Auckland and spent most of the day inside. It was a large building and reminded me of the Louvre in Paris. We were going to be there for a couple of hours but one could spend 2 or 3 days and not see everything. We had booked to see a Maori exhibition of dance etc with a M.C who told us the stories behind the dance. We then had a guided tour of the Maori part of the museum. It was all, not only interesting, but exciting as well

I came across a school teacher and a party of young pupils. When I told them I was in the war I was bombarded with questions. It took some time and Jackie and Gemma thought I was lost. In the end the teacher put her arm around me and thanked me for a very interesting conversation.

We picked up Steve from work, poor chap. Had our pre-dinner drinks saw Deal or No Deal and had a burger dinner for the first time. Played cards went to bed exhausted.

Tuesday 1st May

This was to be a shopping day. Time of departure 11 o'clock straight to the shopping mall in Albany. Had our coffee and I was left in a nice comfortable chair to await Jackie and Gemma's return.

There was great excitement ! Before we left we got information from the computer that we had made front page of the local newspaper with a photograph plus story. At last we were celebrities. I told this story to the waiter in the coffee shop and in between serving customers he kept on returning to hear more. He thought it was a great story.

Unfortunately Gemma got a call from Steve wanted to be picked up from work as he was feeling unwell with spells of dizziness. It turned out when we returned home and Steve saw the doctor that he had a severe infection of the ear. The rest of the day was a little confusing but we had our drinks, sausage and mash etc for dinner, saw Deal or No Deal, played cards and I was rubbish and went to bed.

Forgot to say, that when we returned home Gemma, Jackie and I went into Devonport Village to get a bite to eat. I had one of the famous New Zealand pies. The waiter was not as good as he should have been and as we had just said how very good shop keeping service had been. Gemma went straight to the Manager to complain. Ten out of ten to Gemma.

Wednesday 2nd

It was our last day and so it was going to be low key. My only job was to go with Gemma to the Garden Centre and buy the plants that I was to put in the garden as 'Mummies Patch'. Gemma and Jackie were going into Auckland to do some shopping to get Gemma,s birthday present etc etc etc. Steven was a little better. I sat in the garden in the sunshine did "Mummies Patch" and that was the day over. Had our pre dinner drinks, great excitement about shopping, had a parade of clothes etc. Dinner was a Chinese and a game of cards, went to bed wondering what the journey would be like tomorrow.

Thursday 3rd and Friday 4th

The wonderful adventure was over and what a great time we all had but it now had to end. Steven and Gemma came to the Airport, a few tears and we were away by 12 o'clock. Once again the flights were excellent. We had our one night stay in the Airport Lounge Hotel in Singapore. Very sensible as the first flight was 11 hours and second 13 hours. Not easy but nowhere near as difficult as I imagined.

Back home now with great memories I can only end by saying "I will be back"!!

The photo which was printed in the New Zealand local press

My 88th birthday with Jackie and Gemma

The cake

Steven pointed to the bridge from which Gladys jumped to her death

Gladys's grave without a headstone

The town to which Gladys moved from England

Shark diving

My speech at the party in New Zealand, 28th April 2012:

Can I start by saying how delighted we are to be here amongst our newfound New Zealand relatives. What a lovely warm welcome you have given to myself and my daughter in your beautiful country. It all started with a very sad story when I was a little boy and living in Felixstowe and I am now 88. My grandfather's heart was broken when his eldest daughter left around 1924 to come to New Zealand. It even got sadder as the years went by because her letters were full of homesickness. When the fateful letter arrived telling of her death I was in the house and nothing could console my grandparents. My mother who was the sister of Gladys and my grandparents never spoke another word about the whole episode. For years and years Gladys Wood's name was never mentioned. I have to thank my son Martin and my granddaughter Gemma who now lives in New Zealand, for their hard work paid off when some years ago we found a photograph and could now start to look for Gladys Collins and so we are here today meeting each other in such wonderful circumstances. I understand that Desiree was extremely helpful in the search and so a big thanks to you Desiree. From previous e-mail photos and documents I feel that I know you all, but that would be too simple, we all have our separate memories of what has happened in the past many years. I also have to thank Gemma and Steven for organising this party and my daughter Jackie who has looked after me on what we all know is a long journey. I know that I am in the late part of my life but it is my intention to return. I have been in contact with Abigail Wright and we are going to meet up in the near future. Gemma has my e-mail address so if you have a few moments to spare I would be pleased with your contact, I now live on my own after being married 66 years. I met my wife when she was 18 and I was 16. We came from the different side of the track as at 17 she was a trainee classical solo pianist. The war came in 1939 and from the very first day everyone's life completely changed and did not get normal until many years after the war ended. We had four children, eleven grandchildren, eight great grandchildren. I have been looking forward to this visit for a very long time with great excitement and I am now here. I can only say how wonderful it has been, a lifetime of excitement packed into a few days. Thank you for coming and making our trip such a pleasure and delight. I shall carry the memories back to England and you would be surprised at the number of people who are anxiously waiting to hear our story. Once again thank you very much for your hospitality.'

In 2012 Martin went to both Australia and New Zealand. He went to Australia because he emigrated to Australia in the 1970s but his wife Ann was not happy there and within I think it was about eight months they returned. However the journey to New Zealand was of course to see the relatives that both he and Gemma had worked so hard to find. He had the

Martin with New Zealand relatives

same warm welcome that Jackie and I had when we were there, he loved New Zealand and he certainly liked the people that he met. I'm including a photo of him with the relatives.

One or two things have happened in the family. Robbie and Rachael had a baby girl, Phoebe-Rae, she is now two years old and a real live wire. Chris and Emma had a little boy, Flynn, a problem birth which had to be induced and Flynn was slightly less than thirty weeks and slightly less than two pounds in weight when he was born. It did mean tremendous anxieties for a long time as to whether he would survive or not, but he did and is now fit and doing very well. Roland and I continued to have our day at the races. When Mummie was alive we used to go to Cheltenham, but we stay close to home now and do our racing at Goodwood. The last time we went we both won money which was a big surprise and Roland was quite fortunate because he had a very nice win on the last race and that meant we went home extremely happy.

Mummie and I through the years used to spend some time walking in Gadebridge Park where there is a walled garden. It's secluded and catches a lot of the sun and she and I used to sit there in the sunshine and admire the way the garden itself was set out. I have continued to go there on my own regularly to sit in the garden. I take her photograph with me and put it on the seat that we used to sit on. One or two people as they have passed by have mentioned it and I have told them the story of how we both loved sitting in the walled garden. I don't actually feel as though I'm on my own because I have her photograph with me.

The Walled Garden in Hemel Hempstead

I have had to deal with Christmas cards and birthday cards and goodness knows what, it has taken me some time to get adjusted to that. When I looked at Mummie's list of Christmas cards, there were one hundred and five names and addresses on her list and against twenty one of them was the letter L which meant that they would also have a letter. She used to start her Christmas cards in the middle of November and would do some each day and write a letter as well. She was a prolific letter writer, but in those last two or three years or so it was a real struggle for her. She insisted that she did them on her own and so she did right up until the end.

I have a telephone call every Wednesday morning from Olivia, Vicky and Warren's daughter. She is not a little girl now, she is four but she talks like an adult. I have never known a child like her who tells you all sorts of stories and you're lucky if you can get a few words in here and there. I look forward to her call and I think she looks forward to talking to me. She calls me Granddad John and Granddad John is always waiting for that telephone to ring at about ten o'clock on a Wednesday.

I'm coming very close to the end of my story now. Before I finish I'd just like to record one or two regrets for both Mummie and myself. I know that the one big regret of her life was that she never had a brother or sister to grow up with. She did have a brother and sister but they died at a very young age so there was no one with her to confide in, she was an only child.

Recently we've heard that unfortunately Roland's wife Shirley has been diagnosed with Parkinson's disease. As everyone knows, this is bound to cause a great deal of anxiety and it has come at an unfortunate time because this year she has been the ladies' captain at the golf club and that has put extra pressure on her having to do all those sorts of duties which go along with the job. However, as we all know, you just have to take these things on the chin from time to time and overcome them. Overcome them the best way that you can find, realising that life can never be quite the same.

I would say that my biggest regret is that I never had a father. I know that people will be surprised I guess but I never was able to think of a father at all through the whole of my life and that is certainly one of my regrets. I also regret that while I was at school no one took any interest in my sporting achievements at all, nor did anyone come to see me while I was taking the leading roles in the school operettas. The truth is that I was simply on my own.

Mummie and I both realised that it was a really terrible mistake to destroy the love letters that we wrote to each other. Peggy wrote to me every day while I was away and we did read them from time to time and both of us used to say well we both meant every word that was written in them. But there you are, they were destroyed. We just didn't keep any of them; once again how sad, a big mistake.

I have to record that I am somewhat disappointed that very few people come to see me in Elizabeth House, although of course I do travel away to the children and see as much of the family as I possibly can. I also find it disappointing that some people who climb the ladder of success and quite often reach the top tend to forget those people who are left on the bottom rung of the ladder. No matter how much help you give to those people in their time of need, that help recedes in their mind as time goes by until you are completely forgotten. It's sad; however that is how life evolves and there's very little that anyone can do about that.

So my final sentiments return to the wonderful life that Peggy and I had together. In particular the twenty-three years of shared delight through the whole of our retirement. I know there had to be a price to be paid by the one who was left behind. I miss her all the time. It is and has been a very heavy price indeed. When Peggy said to me, 'You won't forget me will you John' and I replied, 'I would never ever forget you', that is what I meant. Never ever forget!